Intentional Community

SUNY series in Anthropological Studies of Contemporary Issues
Jack R. Rollwagen, editor

Intentional Community

An Anthropological Perspective

edited by

Susan Love Brown

State University of New York Press

Published by
State University of New York Press

Printed in the United States of America

For information address the State University of New York Press,
90 State Street, Suite 700, Albany, New York 12207

Marketing by Jennifer Giovani-Giovani • Production by Bernadine Dawes

Cover photograph from *The Amanas Yesterday,* page headed "The People" with a caption reading: "Family portrait: Grandmothers, aunts, parents and child on steps of a community kitchen in Middle Amana. Dress materials were from the Amana Calico Print Factory."

Photograph by Christian H. Herrmann; courtesy of the Amana Heritage Society.

Library of Congress Cataloging-in-Publication Data

Intentional community : an anthropological perspective / edited by Susan Love Brown.
p. cm. — (SUNY series in anthropological studies of contemporary issues)
Includes bibliographical references and index.
ISBN 0-7914-5221-2 (alk. paper) — ISBN 0-7914-5222-0 (pbk. alk. paper)
1. Collective settlements—United States. 2. Communitarianism—United States. 3. Liminality—United States. 4. Community. I. Brown, Susan Love, 1948- II. Series.

HX654.157 2002
307'.0973—dc 21

2001031438

1 2 3 4 5 6 7 8 9 10

Contents

Preface

This book came into being as a consequence of my attending the annual meeting of the Communal Studies Association in Estero, Florida, in 1995. I was especially encouraged by the involvement of so many anthropologists and others who use anthropological theory to interpret experience in community. After hearing some of the papers presented at this conference and attending a second conference in Amana, Iowa, the idea of a book about intentional community from an anthropological perspective seemed almost imperative, and there was great enthusiasm for the project. I, therefore, want to thank all of the contributing authors for their exemplary commitment to writing, submitting, and correcting their papers. Thanks are also due to the Communal Studies Association for bringing together so many of us on an annual basis to renew our enthusiasm in community with one another.

Jonathan G. Andelson and Lawrence E. Foster made special contributions in reviewing the introduction and some of the papers in this volume. The people at SUNY Press have boosted my faith in the publishing industry through their efficient and congenial guidance of this edited volume through its paces. They have been a pleasure to work with. Much thanks are also due to the Amana Heritage Society and its director, Lanny Haldy, for their permission to reproduce the cover photograph.

We hope that readers, both students and scholars, come away with a deeper appreciation of the role that intentional communities have played in the United States and the role that anthropological theory plays in helping us to understand all societies, including our own.

1

Introduction

Susan Love Brown

In the late twentieth century, the resurgence of interest in community—specifically in the form of communitarianism—served to alert us that U.S. society was engaged in a cultural transition with which many people were having difficulty. Ideologies, reform movements, and even new theories are almost always the result of confrontation with new problems in complex societies, and in the United States those causes were most recently set off by the cultural revolutions of the sixties and the reactions that set in during the seventies and eighties as the generation that carried those ideas matured and took the reins of society. But concern with community and community building is not a new phenomenon—rather it marks U. S. history with a regularity that corresponds to past difficult changes in this country and the rest of the world. However, with a renewed interest in community, and a rich history of communitarianism within the United States, we stand to learn a lot about ourselves and the way in which community functions within complex societies, or the nation-state. Because anthropology in the last ten years has turned its project to focus equally on Western nation-states, this study is even more appropriate.

The project of anthropology has always been to learn as much about people as possible, but this project (being Western in origin) was primarily focused outwards towards those cultures and societies that held both fascination and mystery—that caused us to both question our own values and to enlighten ourselves about the ways in which others saw the world and imagined their place in the realm of being. After nearly a century of systematic study of others—after the generation of theory and the correction of theory—anthropological eyes began to turn back toward the cultures and societies of the West, both critically in order to come to terms with our own past of conquest and colonialism, and to look with new eyes upon ourselves and others. Perhaps of key significance is the fact that it became acceptable to study Western societies (and not only those on the periphery or those minority subcultures considered distinctive) in their great variety and complexity and to begin to apply the same theories and principles to them as anthropologists had long applied to others.

This book is part of that new anthropological project that attempts to apply anthropological theory to elements of Western society—in this case, to examine historic and contemporary intentional communities within the United States for the purpose of trying to understand both these communities and the larger nation-state of which they are a part. The focus on community is at once theoretically and methodologically inspired. Anthropologists have long focused in their unique kind of field research on manageable units of people within larger societies (for example, see Redfield 1960). Methodologically, the study of people in community makes sense and provides some basis for later comparative work. Theoretically, the study of community acknowledges the inherent need for connection that exists among human beings (making communities a naturally occurring phenomenon) and affords opportunities to understand how this need is culturally configured and reconfigured with other human requirements in the face of change.

But community is a complex concept—"a social group of any size whose members reside in a specific locality, share government, and have a common cultural and historical heritage"[1] or "a social group sharing common characteristics or interests and perceived or perceiving itself as distinct in some respect from the larger society within which it exists." Communities can be distinctly concrete or material when defined primarily by their location in space, their use of territory, and the actions and behaviors of their members that yield material forms, such as the building of houses and tilling of fields that create boundaries readily recognized by the members and the public. Community in this sense has always been identified with geography and locale.

On the other hand, community is also a term used in the abstract to denote connection with others—a sharing, sometimes of evanescent qualities, as in *a community of like minds* or *a community of spirit*. Such meaning cuts across boundaries such as space and time and broadens our understanding to encompass those connections that are not so limited: common histories, common practices, common understandings, and common identities that seem to prevail no matter where we go or what we do. Such community seems without limit, for we can imagine a human community that embodies all human beings from the beginning to the end of human existence.

The key element of community, then, lies in how we demarcate the boundaries of the particular communities of which we speak. While all human communities contain elements of the abstract form of community—of psychic and emotional connection—those communities discussed in this book are almost always demarcated by boundaries in space and time that are clearly understood by members as well as those outside the community. In this respect, intentional communities—those consciously formed with a specific purpose in mind—are a natural object of study for anthropologists. Although there have always been some anthropologists interested in intentional communities (see Spiro 1970 on the Israeli kibbutz, for example), the current critical interest by those who have contributed to this volume arises in the midst of a renewed interest in communitarianism—the creation of community—among the public generally.

Present-day communitarianism in the United States takes two forms: it can be seen both as ideology and as action (praxis) in the form of community building. Although this volume is concerned primarily with community building in the form of intentional community, it is worth noting and understanding the ideological form of communitarianism that resurfaced in the United States beginning in the 1980s. Communitarian concerns reasserted themselves and reached visibility with the publication of *Habits of the Heart*, a sociological study (1986) by Robert Bellah et al. concerned with the possibility that "individualistic achievement and self-fulfillment that often seems to make it difficult for people to sustain their commitments to others" might have gone too far and eclipsed other important values of American society (Bellah et al. 1991, 5). This study, which probed both the nature of organizations and individuals, pinpointed a kind of malaise that had been building up for some time and centered the problem on American ideology gone off course, leading to a lack of connection both among individuals and the institutions that benefit the individual and society (see Brown 1991). *Habits of the Heart* was followed by *The Good Society* (1991), in which the same authors introduced readers to more thoughts on ways in which the problems facing Americans might be remedied, emphasizing the revitalization and reconfiguring of American institutions and our participation in them.

These two sociological studies set the stage for a more pointed communitarianism, which took a more definite ideological form in a series of books written or edited by Amitai Etzioni, including *The Spirit of Community* (1993), *Rights and the Common Good: The Communitarian Perspective* (1995), *The New Golden Rule* (1996), and *The Essential Communitarian Reader* (1998), as well as works by others. Communitarian ideology, in the words of its most visible supporter, Etzioni, has a goal:

> Communitarians seek to rebuild community. However, we do not believe that a return to villages or small-town America is necessary. What is needed, rather, is a strengthening of the bonds that tie people to one another, enabling them to overcome isolation and alienation. Above all, it is necessary to reestablish in communities the moral voice that leads people to encourage one another to behave more virtuously than they would otherwise. Communities need to foster civility—a sense of social order and mutual consideration. . . ." (1995, iii)

Communitarianism in this sense goes beyond the academic approach of Bellah et al. It is a broad-based ideological program for recapturing something that Americans feel they have lost, but it is primarily a program of intellectuals suitable to the current social climate in which a great deal of economic stability allows for deliberation about what constitutes a good society. Ideological movements, such as communitarianism, generally originate with intellectuals who are sensitive to changes in society. Intellectuals have often been the harbingers of things to come, but they also often interpret the experience and the particular desires of the general public through their own particular lenses.

Even when communitarianism is based on shrewd observation and an attempt to genuinely solve a perceived problem, such as current communitarianism is, it is more an intellectual blueprint than a plan of action. And even when there is a plan of action, that plan is often systemic, seeing general problems and requiring an overall change of the entire society in order to solve the perceived problems but often not paying much attention to the specific problems of small groups of people. Contemporary communitarianism occurs in the absence of deep societal stresses and, consequently, at a low ebb for community building in the form of intentional community.

Communitarianism as community building—the founding and persistence of intentional communities—although it occurs throughout American history, tends to cluster numerically in times of extreme stress caused by cultural confusion, usually generated by radical changes in the social and cultural environment. The intentional community is one that is purposely and voluntarily founded to achieve a specific goal for a specific group of people bent on solving a specific set of cultural and social problems. The goals of intentional communities vary as much as the people who found them, and they represent the views of small numbers of people. However, these small numbers can reach such a critical mass that the founding of intentional communities becomes a solution to the problem of an increasing unrest. Fashioned according to the needs and beliefs of their founders and subsequent members, these communities help to resolve issues that do not affect the general public as critically.

Intentional communities represent a kind of "voting with the feet"—a call to action that is personal and communal, bringing together the needs of the individual with those of other individuals, reestablishing the bonds that connect human beings but in a particular fashion. The members of these communities often see themselves at odds with or needing to withdraw from the larger society; however, that withdrawal occurs within the context of the larger society.[2]

The intentional community is a phenomenon of the nation-state and an important object of study, because it allows us to observe how human beings living in large, heterogeneous societies use community to cope with the exigencies of life. Although nation-states often consist of millions of people, they do not operate only on that mass level. What make the larger social entity possible are the smaller communities that continue to offer the face-to-face existence that is at the heart of human experience and necessity.

Most of these are "natural" communities, consisting of blocks, neighborhoods, small towns, and so on, into which people fall without much conscious thought, and they make the larger society possible. But these natural communities are integrated into the larger social whole and are seen as a part of it, while intentional communities are more often conceived of as separate from the larger society. When people in mass society face difficulties in making the human connections necessary to sustain them—or when the rules and understandings that once served them well no longer apply—they turn away from their existing communities and toward intentional community with an eye toward setting things right in a more intimate setting. This book examines the phenomenon as it has occurred in the United States.

Although intentional communities constitute a worldwide phenomenon that is as old as states themselves, Benjamin Zablocki, in his book *Alienation and Charisma* (1980, 31–40), identifies four periods of community building in the United States preceding the most recent. The first occurred during the colonial period (1620–1776) and included the Plymouth Colony, the Amish, Labadists, The Ephrata Cloister, the Moravian Brethren, and the Shakers—all groups who left Europe in order to find the freedom to practice their own religions without fear of persecution. These community builders who dissented from the traditional religions of England, Germany, Switzerland, and France established a tradition of intentional community strongly linked to religion and religious freedom that continues to this day. Millennial and mystic visions in religious form are often melded to intentional community, and it is often difficult to separate studies of these religious groups from studies of the communities in which they reside (see Cohn 1957).

A second period of communitarianism was sparked by what Zablocki calls "the Shaker Influx" from 1790–1805, when Shaker colonies swelled with Americans, causing expansion of the established colonies, along with the establishment of other communities as well.[3]

A new century brought with it the third period in which community building clustered in time—the so-called Utopian Socialist Period from 1824 to 1848, famous for the establishment of historical communities upon "utopian" ideals, including New Harmony, Brook Farm, and Oneida.[4] These communities arose in response to economic and social upheavals within the United States as the country moved from an agricultural to an industrialized nation and from a largely rural to an increasingly urban way of life. These communities experimented with new modes of living that deviated in substantial ways from those of the larger society; they were sometimes built upon religious convictions, but also upon social and political ideologies that captured the ideals of the political moment.

The fourth period of community building occurred as the nineteenth turned into the twentieth century, approximately 1890 until 1915, when socialist and anarchist communities sprang up across the nation and began to take the form of urban communities as well as rural ones. In response to the ever increasing urbanization of the country, massive immigration from Europe, and the confrontations of business and labor, people once again attempted to implement their ideals in the form of intentional communities that served as solutions to the problems posed by a constantly growing and diverse society.[5]

The fifth and most recent period of communitarianism in the United States began in 1965 and continued into the early 1970s. Set off by the radical reassessment of values that occurred with the collapsing idealism of the baby-boom generation—confrontations with racism, war, sexism, and any number of perceived injustices that lent a hypocritical tint to many of the ideals absorbed by boomers—new communities, often encompassing new religions and ideologies, seemed to afford a respite from a world that seemed to be falling apart: a world of parents, life-threatening war, and civil unrest. The number of communities formed in this period exceeds the total number of communities formed in all of the preceding periods of communitarianism in the United States (see Zablocki 1980, 32, 34).

Each of these periods of American communitarianism is characterized by what Zablocki calls "a major social or cultural innovation which fragmented prevailing systems of meaning and value" (1980, 38). Change, then, is the usual catalyst to the formation of intentional communities, one that anthropologists have observed across cultures and have theorized about but have seldom applied to their own societies.

This book turns its attentions specifically to the intentional communities of the United States, then and now, in order to further test theories that apply cross-culturally and to help to bring the United States into the human continuum established by a century of anthropological research and study. Indeed, intentional communities have been studied by sociologists, historians, and practitioners of religious studies and American studies with great alacrity and success. Anthropologists bring to this wealth of material and knowledge an emphasis on the processes of culture—those understandings that are learned, shared, symbolic, and integrated into a pattern that is distinct by virtue of time, space, and the passage of events.[6]

As anthropologists know and students of anthropology learn, there is always a disparity between the real and the ideal when it comes to culture, and this is no less true in complex societies (that is, nation-states) than in other forms of social organization. The job of the anthropologist is to note this disparity and how people attempt to reconcile the contradictions that it creates. It is through the analysis of this kind of reconciliation that new knowledge and new theory are produced and older theories substantiated and their powers of interpretation realized.

Intentional communities have often been called "utopian" communities in the past (and sometimes even today), because people often seek to realize their ideals through these communities. Yet, an examination of these communities tells us unequivocally that they are anything but ideal, and while they are often conceived of as separate, they do, in fact, interact with the larger society, sometimes acting as halfway houses for those temporarily disturbed by social forces and sometimes emerging back into mainstream society because they have tapped into important perspectives with wide appeal. The papers in this collection emphasize the use of anthropological theory to explain the nature of intentional community in the United States, and no theory is more applicable than that of Victor Turner.

Victor Turner's elaboration on liminality and the resulting communitas in *The Ritual Process: Structure and Anti-Structure* (1969) provides a firm theoretical foundation from which to explore processes of community building, as do his other writings (1964, 1967, 1975, 1984). In any society, events arise in which members can experience the dropping of the boundaries of identity in order to connect with others and even form new community-based identities.

In her paper, "Liminality, Communitas, Charisma, and Community," Lucy Jayne Kamau points out that intentional communities are almost always liminal, because their members live in a state of "outsiderhood." Kamau explores the ways in which liminality manifests itself in intentional community—through the rejection of normal economic life, reversals of sex roles, attempts to establish equality and common identity through the use of symbols and rituals, and the role of charismatic leaders.

A successful community generates communitas, according to Kamau, who compares two communities that occupied the same physical space at different historical moments—the Harmony Society under the leadership of George Rapp and the Community of Equality under the leadership of Robert Owen—and the vastly different experiences their members had in terms of the identities they attempted to share in New Harmony, Indiana.

"In Search of Truth: Maintaining Communitas in a Religious Community" focuses on the mechanisms by which members of the community called In Search of Truth (ISOT), studied by Gretchen Siegler, maintain the practices and viewpoints that inspire loyalty to their community and have allowed it to survive for over thirty years and to pass this commitment on to their children.

While many of the communities that formed in 1960s did not last, ISOT, a Christian commune located in northeastern California, has been able to maintain its population and weather many exigencies over the years, including periods when it closed itself off from the outside world. It is the ability to "create and maintain certain social conditions that are amenable to a continuation of communitas values" that seems to sustain them.

Lawrence Foster, author of "Between Two Worlds: Community, Liminality, and the Development of Alternative Marriage Systems," discusses three groups that introduced alternative systems of sex-role models to the United States. He examines the celibacy of the Shakers, the complex marriage of the Oneida community, and the polygamy of the Mormons. Going beyond the caricatures of these experiments, Foster suggests that these communitarians were attempting to "create a sort of Anglo-American ethnicity" in order to "revive their own national roots" in much the same way later immigrants would do, and, in the course of doing so, they created new ways of living.

However, these new ways of living, which ultimately resulted in stable communities that lasted many years, were initially traumatic. Foster calls upon Turner's theory of ritual process to demonstrate that though these three groups adopted distinctly different ways of living, their experiences were similar in process. The period of liminality between the old and the new allowed the groups to weather the social changes that established these ways of life.

Joining Turner's theory to the concept of "borderlands" introduced by Gloria Anzaldua in her book *Borderlands: The New Mestiza, La Frontera* (1987), Matthew Renfro-Sargent comes up with an exciting combination of ideas—marginality and liminality—to explain with poignancy the kinds of experiences that people endure in refugee camps, liminal places where old identities have been lost and new identities have not yet gained.

Looking in turn at Hmong, Palestinian, and Maya refugees and comparing their experiences with people living in the historical American intentional communities of Oneida, Brook Farm, and Hopedale, Renfro-Sargent provides a much-needed juxtaposition that elucidates the commonality of experience between those who are forced to be refugees and those who choose to be refugees, both cast into a liminal state in which they pursue a common quest for identity and negotiate its loss and its reconstruction.

Drawing upon another aspect of Victor Turner's work, presented in *Dramas, Fields, and Metaphors: Symbolic Action in Human Society* (1975), Elizabeth DeWolfe analyzes a negative reaction to intentional community—the mob. Specifically, DeWolfe interprets the social dramas that emerged when two women attempted to retrieve their children from their Shaker husbands in "The Mob at Enfield: Community, Gender, and Violence against the Shakers."

From the perspective of the village of Enfield, the breach centered on Shaker treatment of the nonbelieving wives of Shaker husbands and the mothers' right of access to their children. The Shakers saw the conflict differently in terms of religious tolerance and their right to organize as they pleased. As DeWolfe tells us, "the drama is a process initiated by a breach of a social norm or 'crucial bond' among the members of the community at large." The Enfield incident both confirms and departs from Turner's model and also discourages us from believing that intentional communities are havens apart from the larger society.

Addressing the formation and dissolution of intentional communities, an old problem in the field, Jonathan G. Andelson in "Coming Together and Breaking Apart: Sociogenesis and Schismogenesis in Intentional Communities" presents a new methodological approach to the study of these communities. Intentional communities differ from traditional communities, because they usually have clearly identifiable beginnings and endings. Therefore, studies of the life cycle of communities can be done. Andelson considers a community-oriented approach that produces a more dynamic model of these life cycles and accommodates periods of dramatic disequilibrium at either end of their life spans.

Using the theoretical framework established by Gregory Bateson (1972 and 1979), Andelson explores the processes of sociogenesis (formation of new communities) and schismogenesis (disintegration of communities). These processes are analyzed within the context of a number of intentional communities, including the Community of True Inspiration (Amana), the Shakers, the Rappites, New Harmony, and Oneida.

In an attempt to reinterpret older theory in terms of new concepts, I view the theoretically important phenomenon of revitalization in terms of cultural critique (Marcus and Fischer 1986). Anthony F. C. Wallace's recognition of the role of revitalization (1956, 1972) as an underlying principle of many different kinds of movements in response to change not only represents one of the great insights in the history of anthropology but also offers testimony to the ways in which human psychological needs manifest themselves across cultures and levels of organization, substantiating a pattern of common human need for connection. That Wallace saw the creation of "utopian" communities as part of the revitalization process (something that most anthropology texts overlook), along with the fact that most reform movements probably fell within its purview, illustrates Wallace's breadth and depth of vision.

In my paper, "Community as Cultural Critique," I not only establish that intentional communities constitute revitalization movements but that revitalization is itself a form of indigenous cultural critique of the society in which it arises. By concentrating so heavily on the work of scholars and intellectuals in Western societies, we overlook a more pointed marker of what is happening in the society. Through the analysis of the rise of Ananda Cooperative Village at the end of the sixties using Wallace's processual model of revitalization, I am able to show that Ananda represented one conscious and indigenous critique of life in the United States. Further, by applying Donald Janzen's concept of the "intentional community interface" (1981) to Ananda in order to show the feedback mechanisms vital to the process, I demonstrate how revitalization and critique actually proceed and, sometimes, succeed within the larger society.

The papers in this volume allow the student of anthropology to consider theory and its application in a specific cultural and historical context—that of the United States. Further, they illustrate an important continuity in theory and method in the analysis and interpretation of cultural and social phenomena by demonstrating the applicability of anthropological theory to a recurring phenomenon—the intentional community—in a large, Western society. But even beyond this, the papers in this collection illustrate the endurance of solid theoretical orientations within anthropology and the need to fully explore the application of those frameworks to phenomena not previously dealt with to any extent within the discipline. This collection, we hope, offers a first step in this direction.

Notes

1. This definition and the one that follows are from *Webster's Encyclopedic Unabridged Dictionary of the English Language.*

2. This is not always the case, however. Many of the original intentional communities in the United States were started by people fleeing the more established states of Europe. This sort of flight occurs when the lives of the members of the community are in danger, or when they find the culture in which they reside so objectionable and unnegotiable that they have no choice but to relocate.

3. See Durnbaugh1997 for a more detailed description of the array of societies that existed in the United States during that time. For an overall look at communal societies in the United States, see Pitzer 1997.

4. For an explanation of utopia see Levitas 1990, which examines the concept as taken up by twentieth-century thinkers.

5. A recent book, Miller 1998, focuses on the lesser-studied communities of the early twentieth century before the massive community building of the sixties and seventies began. See also Altus 1997 for an illustration of a different kind of cooperative living that was largely urban.

6. I define culture here according to Mark Swartz's definition of "shared understandings" (Swartz and Jordan 1976).

Reference List

Altus, Deborah. 1997. Student Housing Cooperatives: Communitarianism among American Youth. *Communal Societies* 17:1–13.

Anzaldua, Gloria. 1987. *Borderlands: The New Mestiza, La Frontera.* San Francisco: Aunt Lute Books.

Bateson, Gregory. 1972. Culture Contact and Schismogenesis. Reprinted in *Steps to an Ecology of Mind.* New York: Ballantine Books.

———. 1979. *Mind and Nature.* New York: E. P. Dutton.

Bellah, Robert N., Richard Madsen, William M. Sullivan, Ann Swidler, and Steven M. Tipton. 1986. *Habits of the Heart.* New York: Perennial Library.

———. 1991. *The Good Society.* New York: Vintage Books.

Brown, Susan Love. 1991. Breaking the Habits of the Heart. *Critical Review* 5, no. 3:379–97.

Cohn, Norman Rufus Colin. 1957. *The Pursuit of the Millennium.* Fairlawn, N.J.: Essential Books.

Durnbaugh, Donald F. 1997. Communitarian Societies in Colonial America. In *America's Communal Utopias*, edited by Donald E. Pitzer, 14–36. Chapel Hill: University of North Carolina Press.

Etzioni, Amitai. 1993. *The Spirit of Community: The Reinvention of American Society*. New York: Touchstone/Simon & Schuster.

———. 1995. *Rights and the Common Good: The Communitarian Perspective*. New York: St. Martin's Press.

———. 1996. *The New Golden Rule: Community and Morality in a Democratic Society*. New York: Basic Books.

Etzioni, Amitai, ed. 1998. *The Essential Communitarian Reader*. Lanham, Md.: Rowman & Littlefield.

Janzen, Donald E. 1981. The Intentional Community-National Community Interface: An Approach to the Study of Communal Societies. *Communal Societies* 1:37–42.

Levitas, Ruth. 1990. *The Concept of Utopia*. Syracuse, N.Y.: Syracuse University Press.

Marcus, George E., and Michael M. J. Fischer. 1986. *Anthropology as Cultural Critique: An Experimental Moment in the Human Sciences*. Chicago and London: University of Chicago Press.

Miller, Timothy. 1998. *The Quest for Utopia in the Twentieth Century*. Vol. 1: *1900–1960*. Syracuse, N.Y.: Syracuse University Press.

Pitzer, Donald E. 1997. *America's Communal Utopias*. Chapel Hill: University of North Carolina Press.

Redfield, Robert. 1960. *The Little Community and Peasant Society and Culture*. Chicago and London: Phoenix Books/University of Chicago Press.

Spiro, Melford. 1970. *Kibbutz, Venture in Utopia*. Cambridge: Harvard University Press.

Swartz, Marc J., and David K. Jordan. 1976. *Anthropology: Perspective on Humanity*. New York: Wiley.

Turner, Victor. 1964. Betwixt and Between: The Liminal Period in "Rites of Passage." In *Symposium on New Approaches to the Study of Religion: Proceedings of the 1964 Annual Spring Meeting of the American Ethnological Society*. Seattle: University of Washington Press.

———. 1967. *The Forest of Symbols: Aspects of Ndembu Ritual*. Ithaca, N.Y.: Cornell University Press.

———. 1969. *The Ritual Process: Structure and Anti-Structure*. Chicago: Aldine.

———. 1975. *Dramas, Fields, and Metaphors: Symbolic Action in Human Society*. Ithaca, N.Y.: Cornell University Press.

———. 1984. Liminality and the Performative Genres. In *Rite, Drama, Festival, Spectacle: Rehearsals toward a Theory of Cultural Performance*, edited by John K. MacAloon, 19–41. Philadelphia: Institute for the Study of Human Issues.

Wallace, Anthony F. C. 1956. Revitalization Movements: Some Theoretical Considerations for Their Comparative Study. *American Anthropologist* 58 no. 2:264–81.

———. 1972. *The Death and Rebirth of the Seneca*. New York: Vintage Books.

Zablocki, Benjamin. 1980. *Alienation and Charisma*. New York: Basic Books.

2

Liminality, Communitas, Charisma, and Community

Lucy Jayne Kamau

Intentional communities differ from the society that surrounds them, because they are intentional and because they are communal. Because they are intentional, people who live in them are not neighbors by happenstance; they have chosen to live together. Because they are communal, they share things that neighbors do not normally share, such as wealth, property, labor, food, and sometimes even spouses. These are the obvious and well-known differences between life in communal society and life in normal society. There are often other things that separate communitarians from other people, however, that are less obvious and less well known and are characteristics shared by groups that are otherwise very different. These are the condition of liminality, leadership that is charismatic, and an emotional state known as communitas. Together, these create a way of life that is very different from life on the outside.

Most of us live our lives in normal, structured society where life is routine, predictable, and often a little dull, but stable. Life is stable because our mental and social categories and our institutions are fixed and change very little during the course of our lives. These categories and institutions set boundaries around various aspects of social life through the use of distinctions. Society is composed of distinctions on a multiplicity of levels: distinctions between what is mine and what is thine, between church and state, between work and leisure, between the janitor and the CEO, between Monday and Friday. If all this were not so, it would be impossible for us to function and for society to survive.

Many of the distinctions that characterize the structure of normal life are distinctions between persons. A multiplicity of differences are used to categorize people and to regulate their relationships with each other. These distinctions provide the means for a relatively stable and predictable set of social relations. To persist, normal social life must be, above all, orderly. People can be separated by distinctions of class, of race, of locality, and of occupation in a series stretching to infinity. In the modern world, these differences are often expressed in differences in consumption and of taste and manners, which act as markers of social class, perhaps the most important of all social distinctions (Bourdieu 1984).

In differentiated normal society, people occupy statuses and play roles. Roles, in turn, require masks. The individual is not free to do as he or she wishes, because the social script has already been written. Sometimes a person may not even be free to think as he or she wishes. People are constrained by social regulations and segmented by statuses, and even leisure activities are predetermined by the individual's position in society. Because of such constrictions, no individual is able to make full use of the capacities he or she may have.

LIMINALITY

There are places and times in life, however, when the normal structure of daily life is absent, when the abnormal becomes the normal. These are episodes in which boundaries become fluid and identity becomes ambiguous. Normal regulations fall aside and life becomes dangerous, unpredictable, supercharged, and exciting. Normal society seems to be turned on its head. It is these kinds of conditions that Victor Turner investigated and from which he developed his concepts of liminality and communitas:

> The attributes of liminality or liminal *personae* ("threshold people") are necessarily ambiguous, since this condition and these persons elude or slip through the network of classifications that normally locate states and positions in cultural space. Liminal entities are neither here nor there; they are betwixt and between the positions assigned and arrayed by law, custom, convention, and ceremonial. (Turner 1969, 95)

Social classifications do not apply to people in liminal situations. Liminality is a borderline condition. It exists on the boundaries, in the interstices, or underneath society. Liminal life exists outside the normal institutions or structures of everyday life. In liminal conditions, individuals lose their old statuses and identities. The CEO and the janitor are equals. The rules and regulations of normal life may become deliberately overturned so that what was bad becomes good and what was good becomes bad. Boundaries become blurred, so that church and state may become one, as the sacred and the profane merge. Monday becomes Friday and Friday becomes Monday as work and play are no longer bound by conventional time. In contrast to normal society, liminality is anarchic and dangerous.

In liminal contexts, the constraints of ordinary lives have been removed. The individual no longer need wear a mask. Having been liberated from the constrictions of normal society, a person can be free to express his or her personal interests, preferences, and abilities. Participants are free to be "authentic"—to be "themselves."

Liminal conditions can be found in a number of situations, some of brief duration, some occurring over long periods of time. They include initiations, religious pilgrimages, monasticism, boot camps, revolutionary groups, and intentional communities. In all these situations, life is lived outside normal society and on the margins. In all of them normal social rules are inverted and normal social distinctions are abandoned. In losing their old status, individuals are reborn as something different from what they were before. They are leveled and stripped of their old identities and they are joined together in a commonality. Differences no longer matter, and people are no longer kept apart. Instead, they are bound together.

The correspondence of the rise of intentional communities with the development of modern society is not accidental. Modern society contains a paradox: at the same time that the individual has become increasingly paramount, society has become increasingly restrictive, with social distinctions becoming increasingly fine and social categories becoming increasingly narrow (Dumont 1986; MacPherson 1988; Wagner 1981). This has led to increasing tension in modern life, as individuals come to feel that they should be able to express their capacities, while at the same time finding their lives constricted. The contrast between "artificial" society and the "natural" individual is as old as the Enlightenment, whose philosophes searched for natural law among aborigines in the hope of re-forming what they saw as the artificialities of European society. Twentieth-century philosophes have sometimes come to believe that all society is necessarily artificial and that one must move outside normal society in order to be an authentic person. Society as a whole need not be in crisis for intentional communities to form; for some persons society itself is the crisis.

Intentional communities are nearly always liminal and their members in a state of "outsiderhood" (Turner 1975, 232–33). Conceptually, socially, and physically, they are set apart from normal society with its structured statuses and roles. Sometimes the community is geographically isolated from the world, dwelling in a remote location far from ordinary life. The frontier communities of the nineteenth century were literally on the threshold, having been located on the physical dividing line between nature and culture. Although there is no frontier today, many contemporary communities attempt to achieve the same effect by locating in remote rural areas. Even urban communities, surrounded by other people, usually have some sort of spatial isolation, even if it is only the sharing of a building.

Communities are liminal in other ways as well. There may be a rejection of normal economic life in which members turn away from ordinary ways of making a living and become mendicants or in which all goods are shared among the members. There may be a reversal of sexual rules in which members may become entirely celibate or entirely promiscuous (Foster 1984, 1991). Religion, ideology, and worldview are also likely to be reversals of those dominant in normal society.

As Turner defines it, liminality allows only two significant statuses: that of adept and that of neophyte. Adepts have the knowledge neophytes must acquire, and so they are set apart. They initiate neophytes into the mysteries of the group. All neophytes are subordinate to adepts. Neophytes must obey without question and without complaint. They are to accept what they are taught without question. They are to be made anew, to be reborn (Turner 1967, 99–100; 1969, 95). All are equal: any distinctions of class, race, or other statuses that kept them apart in ordinary life are swept away, and they are united in their common circumstances.

This new identity is sometimes symbolized by the adoption of a common costume. At Rajneeshpuram, in Oregon, both male and female inhabitants wore short hair, loose pants, and tank tops (Palmer 1994, 54). Significantly, Shakers did not develop a distinctive style of dress until the nineteenth century, when the early fervor of the movement had passed. Women wore a distinctive white bonnet and kerchief over a long dress in a dark color, a style that had been part of normal rural society in earlier generations. Male clothing consisted of a white shirt, trousers, a vest, a jacket and a hat, likewise similar in style to earlier rural fashions (Stein 1992, 157–58).

In the same way, the old-fashioned dress of the Community of True Inspiration at Amana, Iowa, and also of the Hutterites is a marker of the distinctive and conservative natures of these communities (Hostetler and Huntington 1980; Yambura 1986). Male members of the Krishna Consciousness movement, popularly known as the Hare Krishnas, adopt the garb of mendicant monks of the Indian subcontinent, while women wear saris (Daner 1974; Palmer 1994, 15–43). Gender distinctions within these last communities are marked, but the separation of both from the outside world is also strongly marked by their clothing. They are set off from the ordinary world but bound to each other.

Charisma and communities

Communal societies are often led by charismatic leaders in the Weberian sense of charismatic (Weber 1978, 1111–20). Religious communities are especially likely to be founded by charismatic leaders, and secular communities with such leadership often has a religious or mystical aspect, as in such communities as Oneida or The Farm. Charismatic leaders are often assisted by close lieutenants, with the majority of the members subservient to the leader and equal to each other in relationships similar to the adepts and neophytes described by Turner for liminal states. Followers, like neophytes, are subordinate to the leader and his or her lieutenants.

Persons with charisma are often characterized by extraordinary feats such as miracles and revelations. They have extraordinary power, not because of any office they may hold or expert knowledge they may have, but because they have special, supernatural gifts.

Charismatic leaders are convinced that they have been chosen by supernatural powers and that they have special missions. This conviction is persuasive, because they speak with fervor and sincerity, and they lead by the power of their convictions. Their followers are similarly convinced of the rightness of the leader and the sacred reality of his or her message. Rhetoric by itself is not enough, however. A leader must show that the message is true. As Weber (1978, 1114) puts it, "Most of all, his divine mission must prove itself by *bringing well-being* to his faithful followers; if they do not fare well, he obviously is not the god-sent master" (emphasis in the original).

Charismatic leaders are, above all, disruptive of normal social relations. They and their movements exist apart from ordinary economic life, ordinary social life, and ordinary family life. Like liminality, charismatic movements are anarchic, disruptive, and dangerous. Challenging normal authority, they are unpredictable, and their ideas often threaten normal society by rejecting it. They are separate from the world. They induce people to drop what they were doing, to leave their normal lives and social relations, and to forsake all to follow the sacred person. Indeed, it is their duty to follow that person (Weber 1978, 1113).

Because the members have left normal society to follow their specially endowed leader, they are most likely to find themselves in a state of liminality. They are outside normal society with its normal social statuses and roles and inside a new and different type of society, one in which previous social positions are forsaken and in which the status of follower of the sacred person is all-embracing. The experience of liminality on the part of the followers, as well as their subordinate status and total dependency, no doubt also enhances the sacred aura and power of the leader.

Such a leader is epitomized in Tenskwatawa, known to Euro-Americans as the Shawnee Prophet. The brother of the more famous Tecumseh, the Prophet spent the first part of his life as an alcoholic. While living in Ohio in 1805, he fell into an alcoholic coma and was believed to be dead. He revived just before he was about to be buried and told a story of death and resurrection in which he traveled to the spirit world and met the Master of Life. The Master promised a paradise of rich land teeming with game, provided the Shawnee and other Native Americans abjured white ways and also their own religious traditions and followed the Master's new ways. Tenskwatawa's message reverberated through the tribes, and he attracted hundreds of followers from throughout the Midwest and from as far away as Iowa and the Great Lakes region, who abandoned their homes in order to be near their new prophet. Challenged in 1806 by the governor of the territory, William Henry Harrison, to produce a miracle, Tenskwatawa replied that he would use his power to darken the sun in mid-June. On 16 June, there was an eclipse of the sun. The Prophet's prediction was indeed baffling, and his apparent miracle made more converts out of former skeptics. When the Ohio settlement became overcrowded with pilgrims, he was invited in 1808 by Indiana Potowatomies to settle along the Wabash River. Without intending to, Tenskwatawa created a communal society (Dowd 1992; Edmunds 1983; Kamau 1994)

Charisma, however, is unstable. It can be lost as quickly as it is obtained. If the leader fails in the group's struggle to survive, if he fails to win battles, if his prophecies fail, if he fails to bring well-being to his followers, then he is not "the god-sent master," and he will be forsaken. Thus the Shawnee Prophet was proven wrong in his prophecy that the bullets of William Henry Harrison's army would not harm his followers at the Battle of Tippecanoe. An angry party of Winnebagos nearly executed him, and he was only saved by his fellow Shawnees. His charisma obviously having deserted him, his power was broken, and he remained an outcast for the rest of his life.

Yet another charismatic leader who lost charisma was Winifred G. Barton, founder of the Institute of Applied Metaphysics, or IAM (Palmer 1994, 105–32). Barton, a Canadian, encountered an alien spirit while doing her laundry and began classes in metaphysics in the mid-1960s. In 1976, she and her husband set up four communes in Canada. Barton had predicted a millenarian apocalypse that was soon to come. A series of increasingly bizarre sexual experiments, plus Barton's increasingly incoherent speeches, led to her husband's taking control and Barton's being admitted to a psychiatric hospital. By 1985, all but six members had deserted the IAM movement.

Communitas

In the leveling process that can take place in intentional communities, neophytes often develop close attachments to each other. Because there are no social distinctions among them, there are also no social masks, and initiates can be free to act as total persons. Relationships can be direct, egalitarian, spontaneous, and based on free choice rather than on social similarity. Such relationships may ignore or cut across the distinctions of normal society, which are now irrelevant. A strong feeling of brotherly and/or sisterly love, what the early Christians called *agape,* can develop. These strong emotional bonds are what Turner calls *communitas*. Communitas can provoke strong feelings between persons who in normal life would never communicate, much less love each other.

The experience of communitas can be dazzling. People can communicate spontaneously on the most basic level for no other motive than desire. The most private elements of the self can be freely and safely shared. Such communion can be a powerful experience. Small wonder that people aspire to its sublimity and, once they have achieved it, do all they can to sustain it.

However, communitas is hard to sustain. Its emotions are fleeting and ephemeral; they are most suited for short-term liminal states such as ritual initiations of the sort described by Turner (1967) or revolutionary uprisings (Turkle 1975). These emotions are harder to sustain in longer-lived phenomena such as successful religious movements, monastic life, and intentional communities, where the routinization of charisma can cause a decline in communitas. In such situations, the attempt to continue the group and its associated communitas may lead to the imposition of internal social distinctions and rules that can result in even greater rigidity than those found in ordinary life, ending in a kind of totalitarianism (Meyerhoff 1975).

New Harmony

Explicitly or implicitly, the feeling of communitas is desired by many members of intentional communities, because it can make the renunciation of the world seem worthwhile. Communities have varied, however, in the extent to which they have been able to achieve communitas and retain it. Some have been very successful; others have failed dramatically. Two nineteenth-century intentional communities that inhabited the same physical space serve to illustrate the difference. They were the Harmony Society, led by George Rapp, and the Community of Equality, founded by Robert Owen. Each was resident in New Harmony, Indiana, in the early nineteenth century. The Harmony Society created the original settlement of Harmonie after moving from an earlier site in Pennsylvania. They spent ten years at Harmonie, after which they returned to Pennsylvania. The British industrialist and reformer Robert Owen bought New Harmony from the Harmony Society in 1824, and his Community of Equality began in 1825. It survived for a scant two years before disbanding in 1827. The two communities contrast in nearly every aspect.

The Harmony Society

The Harmony Society began in Württemberg, Germany, with the preaching of George Rapp. Father Rapp, as he was called, was a weaver, who became influenced by the pietistic movement sometime in the early 1780s and began preaching in his own house shortly afterward. Like many other Pietists, Father Rapp and his followers believed that the evil secular world was coming to an end, and that the millennium was imminent (Littel 1976). Rapp was convinced that God had spoken to him directly (Lockwood 1970, 7–14; Taylor 1987, 5–22). There is no question that Rapp was a charismatic leader. His pronouncements were believed to be divinely inspired, and his orders were to be completely obeyed. His special character was emphasized by his remoteness from daily life, especially after removing to the United States. He kept himself apart from his followers, appearing rarely in public. His sermons were stirring, depicting his followers as saints surrounded by a hostile and dangerous world, and his words were charged with significance (Kamau 1992, 74). After a period of persecution in Germany, the Harmony Society emigrated to the United States in 1805, settling first in Pennsylvania, then in southwestern Indiana, finally returning to a new home in western Pennsylvania.

In moving to Indiana, the Harmonists believed that they were the Sunwoman, "the woman clothed with the sun," foretold in Revelations 12, who fled from the dragon into the wilderness. To the Harmonists, the dragon was the wicked world. Eventually they were to be redeemed by the Second Coming of Christ. They fled the world to make ready for the millennium, and they saw certain worldly events, such as the rise of Napoleon, as evidence that the end was near. To prepare for that day, the Harmonists were to forsake private property and live in harmony together, in obedience to their leader. Life was to be lived in an orderly fashion, because orderliness was godly, while disorder stemmed from the influence of the devil (Arndt 1975, ix–xii; Kamau 1992, 71–73).

The Harmony Society deliberately chose to separate itself from worldly society. Its boundaries were clearly drawn and impassable. Three times the Harmonists built new homes on an isolated frontier. Only a few select persons, most notably George Rapp's adopted son, Frederick, were allowed contact with outsiders, and this contact was limited to business dealings. Only certain sympathetic outsiders were allowed to observe the Society's activities, and many of these persons were hampered by their inability to speak German. As a result, they were guided by one of Rapp's English-speaking lieutenants, through whom the Society's beliefs and actions were filtered.

This extreme isolation and liminality followed from the Harmonists' beliefs. They were preparing for the Second Coming of Christ, when only the godly would be saved. In order to be godly, it was necessary to be separated from the chaotic and evil world. Worldly evil was highly contagious, and contact would corrupt the faithful. They were among the elect, intent on perfecting themselves and on creating a society that would be ready for the millennium. The Harmonists held many religious services, but in fact, everything they did, no matter how mundane, was in service to God.

All members of the Society were subservient to Father Rapp. New members were expected to donate all their property to the Society, in return for which they were fed, housed, clothed, and, most importantly, prepared for the millennium. All members worked for the Society. Only persons recruited from Rapp's home region were allowed to join. German Americans who were attracted to the Society were allowed to live nearby and to transact some business with the outside world for the Society, but they were not able to become members (Arndt 1978, 363–64, 465–66; Hebert 1825, 6).

Most Society members spoke no English and thus were linguistically separated from their American neighbors. Most never left the community in which they lived. They wore a distinctive costume resembling clothing worn back home in Württemberg, the men in pantaloons and jackets, the women wearing gray dresses, their hair hidden under a cap (Taylor 1987, 33). They worked and ate together. They were expected to remain celibate, and most slept in sexually segregated communal dormitories. Families with children were allowed separate residences, but husband and wife could not enjoy connubial relations. Society members jointly shared the fruits of their labor. Since the Society was economically quite successful in all three of their homes, the members lived well, even though they worked hard. The Harmony Society's material success validated their leader's message: he did indeed seem to be the godsent master.

That most Harmonists were not dissatisfied is testified to by the Society's relatively stable membership. The majority remained in the society until death, although no doubt cultural isolation, personal poverty, family ties, and the legal difficulty of severing membership kept some in the fold (Taylor 1987, 35 and see Weisbrod

1980, for a discussion of contracts between individual members and the Society). However, it is likely that most stayed willingly, as accounts by various writers of Society members describe what seemed to them to be a remarkable placidity and docility (for example, see Birkbeck 1971; Faux 1905; Flower 1882; Hebert 1825; Hulme 1904; William Owen 1906; MacDonald 1942; Welby 1966; Woods 1968). Although these accounts must be taken with some skepticism, given the fact that visitors saw what they were supposed to see, observers were remarkably uniform in their descriptions. Writers who were hampered by a lack of German noted the Harmonists' cheerful countenances and willing industry, sometimes comparing them to dumb beasts of burden and finding such behavior incomprehensible. Two outsiders—Robert Owen's son, William, who did speak German, and his companion, Donald MacDonald—spent several months in Harmonie between the time William's father purchased the village and the time the Harmonists left. They had ample time to witness dissension, but saw none. As long as Rapp lived, communitas seems to have prevailed among the Harmonists. It was not until after Rapp's death in Pennsylvania that routinization began to set in and the Harmony Society began to experience serious disaffection.

Harmonist communitas may be inferred from William Owen's description of Harmoniefest (1906, 116–17), a celebration of the anniversary of the founding of the Harmony Society:

> This day the Harmonists celebrated the anniversary of their union into a society. They began with music between five and six o'clock and at 9 they went to church; at 12 they dined and remained together with a short interval until near five o'clock; and at 6 they supped and remained together until after 9 o'clock.
>
> What they engaged in we did not learn as they kept it to themselves, but they seemed to think they had passed the day agreeably, and from any expressions which they made use of, I should conclude that the meeting, from some cause or other, had tended to strengthen the bond of Union subsisting among them. They have now been united 20 years. They transacted no business at the store but many persons arrived on business

and were disappointed as they had not given any notice of the intended holiday before. This the Americans thought they should have done. But they seemed to wish to throw a veil of secrecy over all their proceedings. Before breaking up at 5 o'clock, they marched out of the church in closed ranks proceeded by their music, all singing. They halted before Mr. Rapp's house and sang a piece of music and then dispersed.

The Community of Equality

No such descriptions were ever written of Robert Owen's Community of Equality. Owen hoped to found a secular community in which all members would be equal and in which all would be happy. Neither was ever achieved. Instead, there are numerous accounts, both by insiders and outsiders, of dissension, mutual dislike, constant complaints, and very little harmony. The writings of only one member, William Pelham (1916), indicate any satisfaction with arrangements at New Harmony. Other writers expressed profound dissatisfaction, and they repeatedly blamed other members for New Harmony's numerous problems, most particularly its sour social relationships (see, for example, Bernhard 1916; Brown 1972 Elliott 1994; MacDonald 1942; R. D. Owen 1874; W. Owen 1906; Pears 1933).

Robert Owen was a wealthy cotton-spinner. Born in Wales, his mills at New Lanark, Scotland, became famous for the reforms Owen instituted. In time, Owen became convinced that poverty and unhappiness could not be eradicated under a system of private property and came to believe that only a radical change would bring true happiness to people, all of whom suffered under the ills of the present society. These ills included the inheritance of private property, the class system, organized religion, and a rigid marriage system that was unfair to both men and women. Owen's solution was the creation of small, secular, communal societies in which both labor and profits would be shared (Bestor 1950; Harrison 1969; R. Owen, 1971; Podmore 1907). He hoped to erase the social distinctions of his day and to bring about the Enlightenment state of nature, as the constitution of the earliest aspect of Owen's community, the Preliminary Society, indicates:

> The members of the Preliminary Society are all of the same rank, no artificial inequality being acknowledged, precedence given only to age and experience, and to those who may be chosen to offices of trust and utility. (Lockwood 1970, 85)

While, from hindsight, qualifications concerning experience and officeholding seem to forebode events to come, there is no question that Owen was sincere in his desire to eliminate privilege based solely on social rank. Similarly, his belief that his new "Social System" was best tried on the frontier of the New World, which he saw as a tabula rasa, rather than within the confines of the corrupt Old World indicates a desire for isolation, a geographical as well as a social frontier.

Despite its geographical location, Robert Owen's New Harmony was only weakly liminal. Owen was a missionary, and he invited everyone he met to join his community or at least to come for a visit (see W. Owen 1906 and MacDonald 1942 for examples of Owen's proselytizing). During the community's lifetime people came and went at will. Over half the members were recruited locally and could go home any time they wished. Others could leave the community and return, and many of them did. Curious persons came to visit. Anyone could join, and interested persons came to try out the idea of living in community. As a result, Owen's community never really severed its ties with the outside world. In fact, its boundaries were extremely permeable, and it must have been difficult sometimes to know just who was a member and who was not. For example, Gabriel Rey arrived on 5 April 1826, became a member, and left on 14 April 1826 (Elliott 1994, 1059–66). He was not unusual.

Robert Owen was not charismatic; he was rich. He seemed to be offering a good bargain. People could join without sacrifice, seemingly live in the community without personal expense, and be compensated when they left for any work they had done. Unlike George Rapp, Owen could not lead merely on the strength of his personality or his message. He had to persuade people that what he offered was materially superior to life outside the community.

To make matters worse, New Harmony had not one, but two leaders. The second was William Maclure, also very wealthy, who brought with him a number of educators, scientists, and artists who can only be described as being his clients. Maclure, who had made his fortune as a young man and then retired to become a geologist and a reformer, hoped to inaugurate a new type of education at New Harmony. He planned to establish a School of Industry that would educate boys and also teach them useful trades. He also intended to found general schools for younger children. His followers were to teach in his schools. Like Owen, he was not charismatic, merely rich and powerful. Owen and Maclure began with the highest of opinions of each other, but they soon recognized their philosophical differences. Their attitudes shifted to personal distaste, to vicious slurs on each other, and finally to mutual lawsuits (see Bestor 1950 for a thorough description of life in Owen's New Harmony).

Not only was there no charismatic leader at New Harmony, but at times there was no leadership at all. Immediately after visiting the property and purchasing it in January 1824, Owen returned to England, leaving William and Donald MacDonald in charge. He returned in January 1826, bringing with him Maclure, Maclure's followers, and a number of other people. He left again in May 1827. Maclure, for his part, left in June 1826, and returned in October. He left again in November, returning in May 1827. He finally left for Mexico in December, and never returned (Elliott 1994, xxii–xxiii). Both Owen and Maclure were absent more than they were present.

Each of these men had his own followers, and each had his own agenda. Owen was the founder and financial source of the community as a whole, but within that community was Maclure's Education Society. Unlike Owen, Maclure had followers who were financially dependent on him. Most were not interested in communitarian life. They owed their livelihood to Maclure, and they were responsible to him, not to Owen, although some did later defect to Owen. Their connection with the community as a whole was at best tenuous.

Dual leadership led to conflicting and sometimes shifting loyalties, as members grew dissatisfied with one and joined the other. For example, Robert Owen's eldest son, Robert Dale, was a member of the Education Society rather than his father's community. Members of the Education Society, such as the Frenchman Gaulluame Phiquepal d'Arusmont, who had taught in Maclure's schools in Paris and Philadelphia, fell out with the often irascible Maclure and taught in Owen's competing school. Small groups, fed up with both men, began forming their own communities. At one point, there were five separate communities in New Harmony.

As mentioned, neither Owen nor Maclure was charismatic, but either might have been able to foster a sense of unity had they been able to cooperate, or had one or the other been around for any length of time. Such chaotic leadership meant that there was no chance for any kind of leader-neophyte relationship to develop. Instead, the neophytes were left to fend for themselves, and the community dissolved into a cacophony of competing voices. Such a situation could never lead to a leveling of normal social distinctions.

New Harmony was doomed from the beginning, when the members of the Preliminary Society struggled with their daily tasks and with interpersonal difficulties and eagerly awaited Owen's second coming. His arrival, together with Maclure and Maclure's coterie, only made matters worse. While the Preliminary Society had many problems, distinctions of social class seem not to have been particularly abrasive, most likely because most of the members were drawn from the surrounding area and were farmers and artisans. Maclure, however, brought with him the group that was to become the core of New Harmony's self-proclaimed elite, and their presence exacerbated whatever social divisions had already existed.

In New Harmony, as elsewhere at the time, society was divided into two main categories, called the "higher orders" and the "lower orders" (Botcharow [Kamau] 1989). The lower orders included men who did manual labor for a living: artisans, mechanics, and farmers and their families. The backwoods farmers and artisans of the early Indiana frontier were most definitely of this order. Higher orders were people called "ladies" and "gentlemen." Members of the lower orders sometimes called them, contemptuously, "aristocrats." These were men who either did not work at all, or who did not dirty their hands when they did work. They were large landholders or prosperous manufacturers and bankers who were formally educated (see Wood 1996, 299–305 for a discussion of these categories in the postrevolutionary period). Gentility was not merely a matter of occupation or income; it was also a matter of style and manners (Bushman 1992). Gentility meant being an accomplished actor in one's social role. It meant being at ease in company, being able to carry on clever conversation, and behaving with friendly openness, all of which required self-discipline and training. Vulgar, slovenly, or awkward persons disputed the social harmony that gentility required. Distinctions of class were the target of reformers, including those in New Harmony, but no attempt was made to overlook distinctions in manners.

There was some attempt to assign tasks on the basis of need rather than on social rank in the Community of Equality, but this only led to complaints on the part of elites assigned menial tasks. The duke of Saxe-Weimar described the reaction of a young girl, a member of the higher orders from Philadelphia, upon being told that she must desist playing the pianoforte in order to milk the cows: "Almost in tears, she betook herself to this servile employment, deprecating the new social system, and its so much prized equality" (Bernhard 1916, 439). Sarah Pears, another member of the higher orders, had to do laundry and sewing, and she complained of being "sick and debilitated in body, distressed and disappointed in mind" (Pears 1933, 33). In the end, the lower orders performed menial tasks, and the elites taught, wrote, sketched, ran the community store, went off on scientific expeditions, worked on their scientific projects, and often seemed to do very little for the benefit of the community.

The artist Miner Kellogg, who was a member of the community when he was a boy, in his reminiscences unwittingly pointed out the distinctions between occupations that prevailed in the community:

> After four oclock in the afternoon our school hours terminated for the day: then we strolled around and played in the woods as we liked. One day I was walking with Mr. Parsons [Kellogg's teacher], and stopped to look upon some work men laying the foundation for a new building. One of these work men saluted Mr. Parsons and ceased his work to have a chat. "Well, Professor, you have an easy time of it this hot day, but

> you get just as much pay as we do, and yet we work from daylight to dark, whilst you can stop work at four oclock.
>
> "This *does* seem wrong, that's true," said the teacher, "but there are different kinds of labor, some physical and some mental: each has its value in the social economy. Would you like to change places with me?" "No I thank you, but it dont seem fair any how" and turned sullenly away again to his labor. (Sylvester 1968, 56–57; emphasis on the original)

Rosabeth Kanter (1972) includes the commitment of members as one of the criteria necessary for a viable community. The more sacrifices members make, the greater their commitment to the success of the community. Thus, the Harmony Society's insistence that members turn over all their worldly goods to the Society served to increase the dedication of its members. Belonging to the Community of Equality, however, required very little commitment. Not only could members leave and return whenever they wished, but no one was ever required to contribute any amount of wealth to the community. As a result, the more prosperous members could purchase and consume goods unavailable to the poorer members.

Distinctions prevailed throughout the community and seem to have permeated every area of life. As the community struggled to survive, the quality of food served in the communal kitchens declined. All members were expected to eat communally, but those with an independent source of income were able to buy their own food and eat apart from the others. The duke of Saxe-Weimar described eating turkey and drinking wine at a private dinner (Bernhard 1916, 432). The fare at the communal tables consisted of coffee mixed with boiled rye, a few vegetables, wilted salads, and little milk or butter, while "Mr. Owen, constantly boarding at the tavern where luxurious regale was copiously provided to sell to traveling men of the world and loungers, for money, drank rich coffee and tea" (Brown 1972, 25). William Pelham was invited to a dinner at a doctor's, along with William Owen and several others :

> The table was covered with a profusion of delicacies, excellent coffee, tea, cream, honey, sweetmeat, ham, sausage, &c &c in abundance—But I would not have you infer that this good

> cheer is found in every family in New Harmony—the time has not yet arrived when *all the members* are to fare alike—. (Pelham 1916, 403; emphasis in the original)

Not only was the quality of food better in private, so was the company. Saxe-Weimar repeated the words of an elite woman that "some of the society were too low and that the table was below all criticism," going on to say that "it shakes people of education, to live on the same footing with everyone indiscriminately, and eat with them at the common table" (Bernard 1916, 423). Sarah Pears lamented the "rough uncouth characters here" and found it hard to think of them as her equals (1933, 60).

Social divisions marked leisure activities as well. A community costume was devised, but only the elites could afford the material, and not all of them adopted it (Kamau 1992). While the men's costume was similar to general men's clothing, the women's consisted of a short skirt worn over bloomers that some women, such as Mrs. Pears, found scandalous (1933, 42). A device that normally helps to create and express internal unity instead became a source of disunity and social distinction. Some members of the higher orders wore the costume to the popular weekly balls, setting themselves off from the rest. It was only members of the higher orders who were able to dance the elaborate marches, polonaises, and cotillions that were performed (Bernhard 1916, 431). The lower orders confined themselves to the side, where they read newspapers or danced outdoors, as a letter to the Harmony Society written in 1825 by a local resident member, James Hood, illustrates:

> this eavin thay take a dance I was invited to the bawl rume by one of the party thare seams I understand the pore ones will likely danse outerdoors. . . . (Arndt 1978, 557)

In keeping with the hegemony of the refined, concerts, balls, and musical evenings occurred nearly every day, and such events played an important part in the community's public life. The style of these performances excluded those who had not been trained to perform them or appreciate them. As with other aspects of genteel life, these forms of music and dance marked social distinctions, presupposing as they did a certain kind of upbringing and a certain amount of leisure time. They implicitly excluded the less refined.

New Harmony was rife with social distinctions. No leveling process ever occurred, and attempts to create equality through the use of common dining and shared living quarters failed dismally. Members' outside statuses were not abandoned and may even have been heightened in New Harmony, since the haves and the have-nots lived so closely together. Distinctions of social rank were perpetuated by differential purchasing power in the community store, by differences in dress, by differences in diet, and by differences in community occupation. Resentment was common, but when low-ranking members objected or refused to work, they were accused by their social superiors of laziness and a desire to get something for nothing (Sylvester 1968, 57). The simplest daily requirements of the community, such as providing and preparing food, washing clothes, or milking cows became almost impossible to accomplish. Under such circumstances, no feeling of brotherly love could ever develop, and there could be no sense of communitas to mitigate the discomforts and sacrifices necessary to create a viable community.

Conclusion

George Rapp's Harmony Society and Robert Owen's Community of Equality, although inhabiting the same physical space, could not have been more different. They stand as polar exemplars. The Harmony Society is an example of what to do in order to achieve a long-lived community in which most members are reasonably content. They succeeded in creating a condition of extreme liminality or separation from the world and in the process were remarkably able to create a sense of communitas that lasted for decades. Robert Owen's secular Community of Equality failed to separate itself from the world, and there is no evidence that a feeling of brotherly love was ever achieved. Owen's Community of Equality, with little liminality and no communitas, stands as an example of what not to do if one wants to create a viable intentional community.

Reference List

Arndt, Karl, ed. 1975. *A Documentary History of the Indiana Decade of the Harmony Society, 1814–1824*. Vol. 1, *1814–1819*. Indianapolis: Indiana Historical Society.

———. 1978. *A Documentary History of the Indiana Decade of the Harmony Society, 1814–1824*. Vol. 2, *1820–1824*. Indianapolis: Indiana Historical Society.

Bernhard, Karl, duke of Saxe-Weimar Eisenach. [1828] 1916. Travels through New Harmony during the Years 1825 and 1826. In *Indiana as Seen by Early Travelers,* edited by Harlow Lindley, 418–37. Indianapolis: Indiana Historical Society.

Bestor, Arthur Eugene. 1950. *Backwoods Utopias: The Sectarian and Owenite Phases of Communitarian Socialism in America, 1663–1829*. Philadelphia: University of Pennsylvania Press.

Birkbeck, Morris. [1818] 1971. *Notes on a Journey in America and Letters from Illinois*. New York: Augustus M. Kelley

Botscharow [Kamau], Lucy Jayne. 1989. Disharmony in Utopia: Social Categories in Robert Owen's New Harmony. *Communal Societies* 9:76–90.

Bourdieu, Pierre. 1984. *Distinction: A Social Critique of the Judgment of Taste*. Translated by Richard Nice. Cambridge: Harvard University Press.

Brown, Paul. [1827] 1972. *Twelve Months in New Harmony*. Philadelphia: Porcupine Press.

Bushman, Richard L. 1992. *The Refinement of America: Persons, Houses, Cities*. New York: Alfred A. Knopf.

Daner, Francine Jeanne. 1974. *The American Children of Krsna: A Study of the Hare Krsna Movement*. New York: Holt, Rinehart, and Winston.

Dowd, Gregory Evans. 1992. *A Spirited Resistance: The North American Indian Struggle for Unity, 1745–1815*. Baltimore: Johns Hopkins University Press.

Dumont, Louis. 1986. *Essays in Individualism: Modern Ideology in Anthropological Perspective*. Chicago: University of Chicago Press.

Edmunds, R. David. 1983. *The Shawnee Prophet*. Lincoln: University of Nebraska Press.

Elliott, Josephine, ed. 1994. *Partnership for Posterity: The Correspondence of William Maclure and Marie Duclos Fretageot, 1820–1833*. Indianapolis: Indiana Historical Society.

Faux, William. 1905. Memorable Days in America: November 7, 1818–July 20, 1819. In vol. 11 of *Early Western Travels, 1748–1846,* edited by Reuben Gold Thwaites. Cleveland, Ohio: A. H. Clark.

Flower, George. 1882. *History of the English Settlement in Edwards County, Illinois, Founded in 1817 and 1818, by Morris Birkbeck and George Flower.* Chicago Historical Society, vol. 1. Chicago: Chicago Historical Society.

Foster, Lawrence. 1984. *Religion and Sexuality: The Shakers, the Mormons, and the Oneida Community.* Urbana: University of Illinois Press.

———. 1991. *Women, Family, and Utopia: Communal Experiments of the Shakers, the Oneida Community, and the Mormons.* Syracuse, N.Y.: Syracuse University Press.

Harrison, John F. C. 1969. *Quest for the New Moral World: Robert Owen and the Owenites in Britain and America.* New York: Charles Scribner's Sons.

Hebert, William. 1825. *A Visit to the Colony of Harmony.* London: G. Mann.

Hostetler, John A., and Gertrude Enders Huntington. 1980. *The Hutterites in North America.* New York: Holt, Rinehart, and Winston.

Hulme, Thomas. 1904. Journal of a Tour in the Western Counties of America, September 30 1818-August 7, 1819. In vol. 10 of *Early Western Travels, 1748–1846,* edited by Reuben Gold Thwaites, 53–61. Cleveland, Ohio: A. H. Mann.

Kamau, Lucy Jayne. 1992. The Anthropology of Space in Harmonist and Owenite New Harmony. *Communal Societies* 12:68–89.

———. 1994. Prophet's Town: A Native American Communal Response to Conquest. Paper presented to the Communal Studies Association, Oneida, New York.

Kanter, Rosabeth Moss. 1972. *Commitment and Community: Communes and Utopias in Sociological Perspective.* Cambridge: Harvard University Press.

Littel, Franklin H. 1976. Radical Pietism in American History. In *Continental Pietism and Early American Christianity,* edited by F. Ernest Stoeffler, 166–83. Grand Rapids, Mich.: William B. Eerdmans.

Lockwood, George B. [1905] 1970. *The New Harmony Movement.* New York: Augustus M. Kelley.

MacDonald, Donald. 1942. *The Diary of Donald MacDonald, 1820–1824.* Edited by Caroline Dale Snedeker. Indianapolis: Indiana Historical Society.

McPherson, C. W. 1988. *The Political Theory of Possessive Individualism: Hobbes to Locke.* Oxford: Oxford University Press.

Meyerhoff, Barbara G. 1975. Organization and Ecstasy: Deliberate and Accidental Communitas among Huichol Indians and American Youth. In *Symbol and Politics in Communal Ideology: Cases and Questions,* edited by Sally Falk Moore and Barbara G. Meyerhoff, 33–67. Ithaca, N.Y.: Cornell University Press.

Owen, Robert. [1857] 1971. *The Life of Robert Owen as Written by Himself.* London: Charles Knight & Co.

Owen, Robert Dale. 1874. *Threading My Way*. New York: Charles Scribner's.

Owen, William. 1906. *The Diary of William Owen from November 10, 1824 to April 20, 1825*. Edited by Joel Hiatt. Indianapolis: Indiana Historical Society.

Palmer, Susan Jean. 1994. *Moon Sisters, Krishna Mothers, Rajneesh Lovers: Women's Roles in New Religions.* Syracuse, N.Y.: Syracuse University Press.

Pears, Thomas Clinton, ed. 1933. *New Harmony: An Adventure in Happiness.* Indianapolis: Indiana Historical Society.

Pelham, William. 1916. The Diary of William Pelham. In *Indiana as Seen by Early Travelers,* edited by Harlow Lindley, 360–417. Indianapolis: Indiana Historical Commission.

Podmore, Frank. 1907. *Robert Owen: A Biography*. Vol. 1. New York: D. Appleton & Company.

Stein, Stephen J. 1992. *The Shaker Experience in America: A History of the United Society of Believers*. New Haven: Yale University Press.

Sylvester, Lorna Lutes, ed. 1968. Miner K. Kellogg: Recollections of New Harmony. *Indiana Magazine of History* 64:43–58.

Turkle, Sherry Roxanne. 1975. Symbol and Festival in the French Student Uprising (May–June 1968). In *Symbol and Politics in Communal Ideology: Cases and Questions,* edited by Sally Falk Moore and Barbara G. Meyerhoff, 68–100. Ithaca, N.Y.: Cornell University Press.

Turner, Victor. 1967. *The Forest of Symbols: Aspects of Ndembu Ritual.* Ithaca, N.Y.: Cornell University Press.

———. 1969. *The Ritual Process: Structure and Anti-Structure.* Chicago: Aldine.

———. 1975. *Dramas, Fields, and Metaphors: Symbolic Action in Human Society*. Ithaca, N.Y.: Cornell University Press.

Taylor, Anne. 1987. *Visions of Harmony: A Study in Nineteenth-Century Millenarianism.* Oxford: Clarendon Press.

Wagner, Roy. 1981. *The Invention of Culture.* Chicago: University of Chicago Press.

Weber, Max. 1978. *Economy and Society*. Edited by Guenther Roth and Claus Wittich. Berkeley: University of California Press.

Weisbrod, Carol. 1980. *The Boundaries of Utopia*. New York: Pantheon Books.

Welby, Adelard. [1821] 1966. *A Visit to North American and the English Settlements in Illinois*. New York: AMS Press.

Wood, Gordon S. 1996. The Enemy Is Us: Democratic Capitalism in the Early Republic. *Journal of the Early Republic* 16:293–308.

Woods, John. 1968. *Two Years' Residence on the English Prairie of Illinois.* Edited by Paul M. Angle. Chicago Lakeside Press.

Yambura, Barbara S., with Eunice Willis Bodine. 1986. *A Change and a Parting: My Story of Amana*. Ames: University of Iowa Press.

3

In Search of Truth: Maintaining Communitas in a Religious Community

Gretchen Siegler

This chapter makes use of Victor Turner's (1969) model of social relations to explain the commitment of the members of an intentional religious commune known as In Search of Truth, or ISOT.[1] Turner's perspective of the transformation and institutionalization of religious movements facilitates a framework for the collection and interpretation of how practices and viewpoints have changed throughout the life of the group and have allowed it to survive for over thirty years and retain many of its original members, as well as many of their children who are now adults. But it also provides an insight beyond a general evaluation of the community's success, addressing the processes that determine success and the complex interplay of social organization and religious beliefs, both of which serve to enhance commitment.

Victor Turner's Model of Social Relations

Turner (1969) adheres in some ways to Max Weber's (1968) explanation of the "routinization of charisma," agreeing that the charismatic attributes of a group that brought members together in the first place may eventually disappear as the group becomes increasingly institutionalized through time. But he does not believe that this is always the case. He contends that some religious groups are able to maintain these attributes intentionally, ensuring continued success without becoming established denominations.

Turner's model illustrates the two opposed and interdependent modes of social relations. He describes social life as a dialectical process that alternates between states, or "structure," and transitions, or "anti-structure," otherwise known as communitas. Structure is defined as "the patterned arrangements of role sets, status sets, and status sequences consciously recognized and regularly operative in a given society, and closely bound up with legal and political norms and sanctions" (Turner and Turner 1978, 252). Structure is static, hierarchical, and instrumental. Communitas, however, is spontaneous as opposed to normative, affective as opposed to pragmatic, and egalitarian and undifferentiated rather than hierarchical and segmented into status and roles. It is not a mirror imaging of structure, but an intermediate phase between structures. It serves as a liberation from the normative constraints of structure because it relieves the contradictions that are inherent in structure and induces individuals to think about cultural experiences. This causes "periodical reclassification of reality and man's relationship to society, nature and culture" (Turner 1969, 128). In this way it carries members of a group from one culturally defined state to another, from one structure to another.

Turner (1982) asserts that communitas in social relations is made apparent on an individual basis during the experience of Van Gennep's (1960) "liminality." This is a transitional phase that individuals move through that is produced by the manipulation of symbols in ritual behavior. It is most often found in traditional societies, but under certain circumstances liminality continues to be found in complex societies (Turner 1969, 167). This can be seen in religious movements that often withdraw to the edges of social structure. They are able to nourish communitas, because ritual and myth, and work and play, are integrated into the total social process affecting the existing social order. These marginal groups are at the "interstices of structure, in liminality; at the edges of structure, in marginality; and from beneath structure, in inferiority" (Turner and Turner 1978, 251).

Turner delineates three types of communitas exhibited by these groups. During "spontaneous communitas," "social relations are simplified, while myth and ritual are elaborated . . . [and it is] a period of scrutinization of the central values and axioms of the culture in which it occurs" (Turner 1969, 167). They are in a phase of openness, have little or no structure, are committed to equality among their members, and do not seek property. Eventually such groups move from spontaneity toward pragmatism as it becomes necessary to become involved in the production and distribution of resources, and to create some form of social control. As they become more structured they exemplify "normative communitas," or "the attempt to capture and preserve spontaneous communitas in a system of ethical precepts and legal rules" (Turner 1977, 46). In time, the balance between communitas and structure becomes very difficult to maintain and these groups are threatened by institutionalization, at which point they often fractionalize (Turner 1974, 81).

Yet successful religious movements exhibit a third type of communitas, which Turner calls "ideological communitas," or the intentional maintenance of communitas, often allowing these religious movements to survive even while becoming highly structured. A complete ideology is created that allows the liminal to continue within the central social process, promoting communitas. During ideological communitas "the ultimate desideratum is to act in terms of communitas values even while playing structural roles, where what one culturally does is conceived as merely instrumental to the aim of attaining and maintaining communitas" (Turner 1969, 177–78). Often, although not always, the ideology is based on apocalyptic mythology where a divine crisis will mark the permanent attainment of this "established mode of being" (Turner 1969, 153–54).

The application of Turner's model

I illustrate the interplay of communitas and structure and its relation to commitment in the ISOT community in the following way. First, I provide a brief description of the beliefs of the group and how they structure their everyday lives in accordance with them. Central to these beliefs, a higher authority calls for them to transform themselves, both individually and as a community, in preparation for a special role at the end of the world. This mythology, within which they must actively participate, has allowed them to establish ideological communitas. Second, I trace the history of the group as they move from spontaneous through normative communitas. I concentrate on those events that have threatened the existence of the community to show how their ideology has allowed them to adapt to their circumstances. Structurally, in response to different situations, they generate new social arrangements, but it is merely aimed at maintaining communitas. They continually evaluate meanings and provide alternative ones by making use of their religious beliefs and their symbols to integrate the liminal into the total social process. In this way, they introduce and reintroduce values of communitas into everyday life. Finally, narratives from the members support these ideas. They provide insight into why they believe that only their religious beliefs provide the level of commitment necessary to live together in community.

Introducing the Community

ISOT is a Christian commune located in Northeastern California.[2] It is an autonomous community formed in the mid-1960s but has its roots in an earlier charismatic movement. This Neo-Pentecostal movement began in the late 1940s when evangelists spread a "Spirit-based" Christianity that differed from traditional Pentecostalism. In 1951, a meeting of the Full Gospel Business Men's International was held in California to provide outreach to non-Pentecostals searching for charismatic fellowship. By the mid-1950s, an umbrella organization called Christian Growth Ministries was formed in Fort Lauderdale, Florida (Burgess and McGee 1988, 130–37).

Through teaching conferences and then a traveling ministry, charismatic pastors were trained to be leaders. Some of these leaders demanded a commitment from participants that was expected to be stronger than that of regular church involvement. It resulted in a scattered network of communes and congregations loosely assembled in an organization that eventually became known as The Body. One of these communes was ISOT. While many of the original groups affiliated with The Body no longer exist, there are still over two hundred active communities in North America. Differences in beliefs caused ISOT to stop interacting with The Body in 1974, but they reinitiated contact in the late 1980s.

The members of ISOT share the religious beliefs taught to them by a woman named Marie. Followers claim that she is a prophet with the ability to foretell events because of a direct connection with God. She can be considered a postmillennialist, or one who believes that we are approaching the final days of the thousand-year period preceding the end of the world mentioned in the Bible. God tells her that a "body" of people who "manifest Christ" will come together and prepare others for this time of transition. Her followers learn that they can be among those who have been "chosen" to fulfill this covenant, but they must prepare themselves.

Their primary goal is to progress spiritually, demarcated by a series of revelatory experiences, both small and dramatic. It can best be initiated, they believe, in a community that heightens social relations so that religion becomes a part of everyday life. In this way, they are able to dedicate themselves to spiritually heal those around them. They hope that as they transform their individual "natures," they will become interdependent parts of a whole with others in the community. At some point a spiritual level will be attained at which they will transcend themselves.[3]

The community has supported itself in a variety of different ways, occasionally barely subsisting but at other times living quite comfortably. It originated on the central coast of California when Marie began holding religious meetings in her home. She converted those who subscribed to her interpretation of the Bible and support of spontaneous religious experience. As members grew in numbers, they bought a hotel, began to live communally, and became licensed as a nonprofit religious organization. A core group provided to anyone in need, pooling their incomes from a variety of menial jobs.

In 1972, ISOT relocated to the northern part of the state and accumulated most of the land within and surrounding a small rural town. Members grew most of their own food, labored for local ranchers and the forest service, ventured in small businesses, and took in foster children. By 1976 they began to educate their own children, and some of the adults were pursuing college educations. They licensed as a Group Home in 1984 and found financial success by providing homes and counseling services for approximately seventy children who were wards of the state. In 1992, they lost this child-care business because of charges of child abuse. Forced to change their lifestyle dramatically, they now work in a variety of jobs throughout the region, some in professional positions and some in successful contracting businesses.

The community has maintained a fairly stable population of approximately two hundred members, most of whom live communally. Families share life in six clusters of buildings; a main house serves as a dining and living area, and nearby structures provide bedroom quarters. They frequently move from one cluster to another to avoid becoming too attached to any set of individuals. Children used to have their own separate cluster, but now many live with their parents. While it is expected that everyone will live together in concurrence with their religious beliefs, some marginal members maintain their own homes on the boundaries of the commune. A few, who are unable to live with the group but are also unable to live alone, are given private trailers temporarily with an understanding that they will try to assimilate with the rest of the group. Everyone is expected to come together at a central meetinghouse for at least one meal a day and for social and religious activities.

Members believe there is an order of authority presented to them in the Bible and members should follow these prescriptions. In the family men are considered "the law" and women are expected to implement that law. Age is also considered in the prescribed order. Those who are older must be submitted to, although ideas of spiritual progression may supersede these requirements. Children should always listen to those older than they but can always go to someone if they do not agree. In the community, women can have position over men based on their spiritual gifts. The titles of "Elders," "Timothys," members, and affiliates characterize positions in the religious hierarchy and usually, although not always, parallel positions in the operation of the business affairs of the community. Most of the Elders, or leaders, have been in the community for a few decades. They give spiritual guidance to other members and also supervise various aspects of community life. Their spiritual advisor is Marie, who consults about religious affairs, although she has managed to transfer many of these duties to other Elders. Her husband Joseph administrates the business of the commune, but he is also a primary leader in its religious activities. A relatively new designation of Timothy was designed to provide training to younger and newer members who hope to become Elders in the future. They take on more mundane supervisory duties. The designation of member is given to most others. They usually are not considered ready to take on too much responsibility, or do not care to be in any position of authority. Affiliates are recent arrivals who must prove to the Elders that they are committed enough to become members.

The ISOT community has had a turbulent history resulting in events that caused its members to periodically close and then open themselves up to outsiders. When they moved to the north, they almost immediately came under attack by their rural neighbors, who thought of the commune as a "cult." Generally the resulting harassment was petty, such as deflated automobile tires and complaints in the local newspaper. But in 1979 a local Pentecostal minister picked up one of their foster children who had run away. Her claims that the ISOTs had handcuffed her to a bed led to a TV news series speculating about possible child abuse in the commune. The charges were never substantiated, but the ISOTs concluded that the values and actions of these neighbors threatened their existence as a group. For protection, they established boundaries and generally closed themselves off from outsiders. They allowed only that outside scrutiny necessary to continue their child care.

In the 1980s, total reliance on taking care of children on their property in a Group Home brought them financial stability, but also left the commune in a period of turmoil. The state of California desperately searched for anyone willing to deal with children who were one step away from Juvenile Hall. The ISOTs had the expertise, credentials, and facilities necessary for this endeavor. In addition, this work coincided with what they believed was their calling: caring for the downtrodden. But the operation of such a facility on their property demanded that they separate their religious lives from their everyday working lives. Some core members found this separation contradicted their original intentions for living in community—to immerse themselves in their religious beliefs.

Total reliance on the Group Home for financial stability, they also worried, made them once again open up to the wider community, threatening their beliefs and autonomy. So a number of members, who so many others depended on, decided to leave. The timing of their departure was detrimental because of a coinciding investment in a large piece of property. The number of people on hand to run the new Group Home was reduced, and outsiders were hired for staff positions, reducing the profit potential. Yet the commune managed to survive this crisis and slowly gained the respect of the wider community as major employers in the lucrative business of child care.

The early 1990s brought another upheaval when more severe accusations of child abuse forced them to relinquish their control of the Group Home. This time the charges included psychological, physical, and sexual abuse and were directed toward central, long-term individuals in the group. Accusations came from children they had cared for in the past and from a man working undercover for a state regulator committed to close down most Group Homes in California.[4] But most damaging and painful were the accusations that came from some disgruntled ex-members who had left with that core group in the early 1980s. They had left on bitter terms because they had forfeited the personal investment they had made in the community over the years. A few also happened to be closely related to central figures in the group, including Marie.

Three choices were available to ISOT. A plea bargain would allow the group to retain the Group Home, but the accused would have to assume guilt and have no future contact with children. A lengthy trial would allow them to defend their reputations but also force them to publicly air family matters and ruin any future reconciliation with their relatives. They choose the third alternative: to close the Group Home and start over.

This final crisis threatened their survival and made them realize that they could not remain isolated from other groups with similar beliefs. Some members could not bear the strain of uncertainty about their economic future and left. Those who remained needed the support of friends and found it by reinitiating contact with The Body. Other affiliated communes within this wider organization started sending them families who had children who were troubled. This new membership swelled the ranks with people who needed support, but it also rejuvenated the community. By 1994 newcomers were being turned away for lack of space.

Successful commitment

The members of ISOT agreed that even while various crises throughout their history caused some to leave, those who remained were strengthened because they were forced to periodically reevaluate their beliefs. Regardless of the external turmoil, and maybe in part because of it, they knew that the end of the millennium was near. It meant preparing themselves for their calling as God's chosen and directed them to work to transform themselves spiritually to fulfill this role. Reminded of these shared goals, their emotional bonds were enhanced, renewing their commitment to the purpose of the communal environment. Its closeness forced members to help each other change, so that they could become interdependent parts of a whole. Only then, they believed, would they be unified and fulfill their covenant with God. In this way, crisis led to a renewed sense of their core beliefs, which lead to beneficial changes in the group.

Joseph explained the importance of their religious beliefs to their communal experience. He explained how the changes initiated by being "born again," that first revelatory experience thought to be necessary for further spiritual progression, helped them live together:[5]

> First of all, the Scriptures give us the words to help us explain the experience we're experiencing. So without that image, and without that explanation that this is who we are, this is what life is about, this is why we're experiencing this, this is what we're struggling for, we would have to find our own explanations for what we're experiencing. That is the cognitive part. Then the emotional part is that how are any of us ever going to transcend our essential selfishness if we aren't a new creature

> in Christ. Separate from that rebirth experience that we believe is fundamental in a Christian life, we're just common-minded human beings who are primarily motivated to live strictly for ourselves. It's the only way we transcend that as being our primary point of reference. So being born again is a shift from where before your primary point of reference is yourself. . . . you are the center of your own world and it's really up to you how you shape and define that world. What being born again does is it allows you to place God in the center of your life and put your life in perspective where you're not the center. It may be very discomforting to some and comforting to others.

Some members, more than others, exemplified these religious values. Even as an outsider, I was aware of those who were committed to the community simply through their daily actions. These members tended to be consistently available, devoting most of their free time, not just physically but emotionally, to others. Invariably these same individuals were comfortable and proud when they expressed their religious beliefs to me. Marie explained that these people had internalized the values of the group.

Those individuals were most often leaders in the group, but not always. Most of the leaders tended to be long-term members and, therefore, had shared in the development of the goals and values of the group. Those who came later were attracted to the group because of their conversion experiences but had not completely identified with it. One member pointed out that as an outsider I might agree with someone on issues, but for different reasons depending on our personal agendas, while committed members agreed on issues for the same reason, because of the goals of the group. Janine gave some insight on their shared purpose for living in community:

> Well I think that you can only live here if you know that you're supposed to be here. . . . if you know God has directed you here. I think it takes more than just wanting to live with people. It takes a relationship with Christ and wanting to grow spiritually as well as physically and mentally. I think you have to have a purpose for being here. You can't just live here for the soup kitchen.

Dick explained further how the same goals made them willing to invest in the community:

> If you are here after the age of eighteen, it is assumed that you are here to seek out an understanding of our religious functions and who we are as a religious people. It's not just a place to live and a place to eat and a place to stay. You are looking for a relationship with God and listening to the teaching and the ministry. It's actually more of a commitment, and of course you are free to leave anytime you need to. You understand that if you stay here, you are making a commitment to keep the rules of the society and look for more of a relationship with God. People have to come and feel like they can invest. . . . that it can be equally theirs along with anybody else's. It's kind of like in the kitchen. If everybody feels like it's theirs, the job is a lot easier. But if everybody doesn't feel like it's theirs, what would they want to invest? And people have to invest you know. They have to make this whole thing theirs. We want that because we realize it is such a big job that has to be done. We are not going to do it all by ourselves, or as the little part of a Body that we are. Us having the same goal—this is what makes this community strong. So I would say to anybody who wanted to live with a community—have the same goals.

Living in accordance with their religious beliefs was of utmost importance to most ISOT members, but they also found it easy to discuss other benefits that they accrued from the experience of living together. Most did not believe that humans were meant to live alone; they thought they should have a support system. Few spoke of the material support, while many mentioned emotional security and how important it was to have help raising their children. Misty spoke about these benefits in individualistic terms, contrary to how she and most others usually speak about their lives:

> I would probably focus more on the family aspect of it. The benefits of living not just for yourself, but for your spouse and for your children—all the support that you end up getting. My sisters have told me more tales about trying to find someone to watch their kids and all the things that they don't get to

> do because they're basically stuck—bad experiences they've had with people watching their kids, bad experiences they've had in general. A lot of those things I haven't experienced. If I go to work, I have someone that watches my kids or cooks the meal or does the laundry. It's hard to get people to understand that because they're so used to being by themselves. I would also focus on the strength that it gives you, not just literally, but spiritually. The communication that we have. We don't have people that go around that are upset or angry, or they see you coming and everybody shuts their mouth because they don't want to tell you how mad they are with you. If we have a problem with each other, we talk about it.

Kara offered her perspective:

> I live here because this is where God sent me to live. I didn't just choose it because it's the best community, although I think it is. I've been to a few others, even lived in some. The most meaningful aspect of it is just having the support of the family—knowing there are other people around. I wouldn't know how to separate myself from them very well now. I mean I could, but it just wouldn't be the same. I like the benefits that my children have with people that I can trust. If I lived in a neighborhood, the neighbor down the street might have some impact in my kids' life that I don't want. When I was younger, we even had a lot of people around, but they didn't really help raise us. My kids are freer and happier.

Accepting the less committed

The ISOTs had periods when they loosened their boundaries to outsiders, but until the 1990s, it was expected that those who lived with the group would totally commit themselves to its principles. A message at a Sunday meeting told them that they were not "30-fold" and, therefore, must avoid the notion of "part-time stuff for me and part-time stuff for the community." Those who could not share the goals of the group were regarded as threats to its unity and expected to seek counseling. As in most groups that have been together for a long time, those who had made long-term sacrifices, and those who were more committed, accorded the less committed low status. Helen acknowledged how they could make it difficult for newcomers to adjust:

> We have twenty-five years of experience behind us that have made us who we are today and that have made us as close-knit as we are today. We wouldn't be who we are without those experiences. People become intimidated by that. Its been very difficult having to find ways to help them integrate into the family experience and not be put off by "Oh, I'll never get to be inside." We've had people come and go over the last few years. Some people have used that as an excuse. Other people have said, "I want to be a part of my own experiences with you." They're the people who have really gotten in and become a part of the family. They're finding that the experiences are there and found a place themselves that makes them just as much a part of us as people who were here twenty-five years ago. They can share with that kind of vulnerability and they weren't intimidated at all. They've been able to bridge that because they wanted to be a part of it.

The group came to recognize that rigidity not only could create separation within the group but also isolate the commune, threatening its survival. Perceptions of vulnerability after the child-abuse allegations made them decide that the community could no longer stand alone. In order to reestablish relationship with others in The Body who held somewhat different ideas, they had to become far more inclusive than in the past. Evelyn illustrates how they had changed:

> I think we have to be a little less quick to judge and check out where people are coming from and what they mean. We have to be a little more careful about saying, "I want to tell you this—maybe it'll help what you're doing," or "I really don't like that. I'm not comfortable let me tell you why." We need to give people a chance for us to see what's going on. We're pretty dogmatic. We went through real dark ages where it was "do it our way and that's the only way it's right."

Joseph reflected on some of the benefits that accrued from this new openness to other ideas:

> If you look at all of life as a learning process, as a developmental process, there could be little doubt we had been fairly isolated from other communities for a number of years. There was a certain, maybe you could call it provincialism, or something. I don't know what the right word is. The experience of going through the problem with the Group Home and having to search for different ways of earning a living, certainly opened up a lot of reuniting with the larger group that had other community contacts. Bringing people into the community from those contacts—there's no such thing as being unimpacted by their presence. Just the process of you coming asking questions—getting people to think about what they were doing. We've had a greater need to look inside of ourselves and explain ourselves. The increased need to explain ourselves and to put our twenty years of being together in a context that other people could understand has created maybe a little more insightfulness—maybe a greater ability to communicate than we had before. I think as you gain ability to communicate who and what you are and what you're doing, you gain more peace about it. If there's something you couldn't explain, you might review it and say, "If I can't explain it, maybe I shouldn't be doing it." I don't think any community is static. There's no steady state.

Everyone in the community had the opportunity to broaden his or her perspective because of these new, outside relationships. Misty explained how she was changed:

> I think going on the trip [to visit other communities] was a real eye-opener for me. It's easy to get stuck on the idea that we're the only ones that live this way. Seeing how many thousands of people there are with the same kind of focus in their lives, seeing the multitudes of God's people that He spread out all over. Plus the fact that the people that have come are in need of prayer, or people that drive through and they stop and

> they visit. It makes you see that there is so much more happening. We're like a tiny little speck. You wish you could say you were the cake, but you're just a little speck of the frosting. It's just a little piece that we're going to give and add and be. I think the one thing that really hits me is to not break fellowship with other people just because someone doesn't believe all the same things that you believe. Just because someone isn't living the same way you live, you shouldn't break the fellowship that you can have in Christ between you. Hold onto that.

The ISOT's increased willingness to allow people with different levels of commitment to live with them was difficult for some long-term members, despite their good intentions. One of them, Dick, commented:

> Hopefully if they are here, they will really want to be a part of this forever. If not, then hopefully they will get whatever they need here and then go where God really wants them. Of course we don't just say, "Why don't we have everybody come here we know?" Every family that comes, we talk about it, and what we try to do is take the people we really believe that God is sending to us. It's kind of like what we have with each other is like a marriage really—a fellowship. It's like a lifetime relationship that we have with each other and we expect that people that come here would have that kind of relationship with us. We want to make it as big and as much room for anybody that wants to stay here.

Diane supported Dick's position, probably because so many had taken advantage of the group in the past:

> It's like an extended family. If you want to be a part of the family, their heart is open to you. But if you're just going to live here and receive and never give . . . even in a home a parent would say, "Hey, you don't want to live by these rules—you don't want to give and be a part of the family. Go someplace where you do feel comfortable."

Questioning commitment

While individuals had different levels of commitment, the uncommitted were in the minority and easily identified. Some left the group and returned periodically. Others attempted to work a normal workweek but did not make themselves available at other times. A few lived in homes near the community but followed a somewhat separate life from the others. The uncommitted often were unable to submit to authority, did not appear to enjoy what they did, and exhibited discomfort with their dependency on the others. This negativity was attributed to a number of factors. Even when every attempt was made to keep channels of communication open, sometimes individuals would become paranoid because, it was claimed, they clung to disagreements and allowed them to fester.

Most of the adults, while admitting that they had on occasion wanted to leave the community, did not like to discuss problems with the life they chose because they tried not to think negatively. Yet some of the problems were apparent. The close living and working quarters created an environment in which every individual action affected others. Certain liberties, therefore, had to be denied. Often vehicles were difficult to reserve, so private matters had to be planned far in advance. One man found life in a commune difficult, because everything had to be done by committee, and everyone had different ideas about how it should be done. Someone else said that, just as in her own family, she often had no choice about who became a part of the community. Yet she maintained that if she had problems with someone's behavior, she certainly could air her views. Many expressed annoyance with the lack of personal privacy. One young adult wanted to have his own space and schedule and not always have to deal with other people's problems. He also tired of having himself "exposed," or discussed publicly, when he did not believe it benefited anyone. Janine agreed:

> Sharing all things in common and living in community, there's a certain amount of privacy that you just have to do without. Everyone gets a certain amount of physical privacy. But people are involved in your life. People wonder how you are, ask you questions, and butt into your life. If you want to live privately this is no place to live.

Those aspects of community life that individuals found difficult were often quite personal. Evelyn tried to think of her reliance on the others as interdependence rather than dependence. But probably because she had never lived on her own, she could never give up the wider societal value placed on independence. Pursuing this underlying desire, she began to work outside the group and found that she could support herself for the first time in her life:

> There's always that feeling to want to be independent. I've gone through a lot of traumas about when do I get old enough to just do things the way I want to do them personally, to my taste. There's a lot of giving up your own personal taste and space. Privacy. That's probably the biggest drawback. I get absolutely nothing financially from the ISOT family anymore. I can decide whether I really what to be a part of people when they can't give you anything. Well, now I want the spiritual things: the leadership, the fellowship, the counseling. I want to be part of the family. My family was always wondering if I was there for them or for the financial security. I'm not dependent on them for anything anymore. But that doesn't change my life as much I thought.

Pat was raised in the group with no knowledge of another lifestyle, but as a new mother she had personal issues involving child rearing:

> I would focus on children, because that seems to be where a lot of the problems happen. A lot of the conflicts with adults happen over raising their children, and whether they are doing it poorly or satisfactorily. You also have to be willing to be touched in every single area of your life, every single aspect of who you are and what you believe in. There are a lot of times where you feel like what somebody is saying is not true to you. If you don't pray about all that stuff and say, "Lord if you are trying to say something to me I want to hear it," then you are going to basically be an angry individual a lot of the time and probably eventually end up leaving the community. I guess I would focus on raising children and what that all means, and that is a hard job especially when there are a million opin-

> ions on how it should be done. You are going to have to have a strong relationship with the Lord if you are going to live in a community.

I asked Pat whether she was ever curious about what it would be like to live with her husband and child as a nuclear family. She replied:

> Honestly, I haven't had too many of those urges. Some women feel like they don't get a chance to do all the things that a wife should do—whatever is their idea of being a wife. I take the opportunity sometimes when we are out, but it has never been a big deal for me to go and have my own home and stuff. I think a lot of times the kids now don't have any idea how much they have and so they become kind of spoiled in some ways. Things become more important than relationships with people. They look out in the world and they see all that they don't get and they want more. It makes it harder to keep your kids, I think.

Even Joseph, an astute businessman with a Ph.D. in administration, admitted problems that he and others were forced to overcome to live together successfully.

> With my talents and education I'm sure I could be earning a lot more money and building a lot better retirement if I were not part of this community. You have to make a commitment that the longevity of the community is greater than yourself. You have to be willing to be involved in some very profound relationships with other people. That can be very threatening and very frightening, because by nature as human beings most of us will allow a few people close to us. We may at times complain about not having a lot of significant people in our lives at a given moment, but the truth is that we get very threatened and afraid when people are too significant to us. . . . when they have too much meaning, and they are too important, and we feel so emotionally tied to them that they become part of our identity. So in order for a community to survive, you have to transcend that. You have to be willing to let a

much larger group than we want by nature to become significant others so that you truly create an extended family—that sense of intergenerational continuity and belonging. In an increasingly transient culture, I think I would have to address the need for permanency in commitment to a relationship that says, "We started this when we were twenty and we fully expect to be in the same cemetery together when we die." Without that commitment there are too many reasons to blow it apart. I think those would be the cornerstones that I would address if I was going to write about community and try to explain it to people who are outside. I'd want them to understand that in order to become a community you have to force yourself to face your own human fears at a very profound level and overcome them. Communities that have a sense of integrity are those that have a commitment to something greater than the sum of the individual and have a vision of themselves as a community.

Adults leaving the community

People who leave the community, particularly those who have been with it for many years, affect both the physical and emotional well-being of those who stay. As mentioned above, the loss in the 1980s of a group of core members who did not want a Group Home only hurt the livelihood of the group for a short time. But the group had made long-term financial and emotional investments in many of them. It had financially supported their college educations with the expectation that they would repay it in future work for the community. In addition, anyone who had been with the group for some time established a deep relationship with others that went beyond mere friendship. It was often described as a covenant similar to marriage and, therefore, the breaking of this covenant had the same emotional impact as a divorce. The resulting pain is evident in a conversation with Dick, who after ten years continued to speak about the loss of this core group:

So many people felt they were going to spend the rest of their lives here. They just decided at different points along the

> way that God called them to be here. But they didn't think that God called them to take care of the Group Home kids. That could be rough for awhile. Then they are gone. I suppose people ultimately wanted something different for themselves and stopped wanting what we want.

Chuck also referred to some of these people, along with others who had left more recently:

> Right now I don't have so much contact because people that have left have made some definite opinions about ISOT. They don't feel like we can communicate. I don't agree with that. So there's been a real cut and dried cutting—not one that I want, their choice. I don't want to make their life uncomfortable for them, because they were part of this for so long. They were my best friends. They decided to go another way, and it really is totally different.

In the past the ISOTs made it difficult for those who wanted to leave. They would be emotionally pressured to stay through confrontation and counseling. If they left, all emotional ties were abruptly broken and they would be given no financial support. But when the Elders came to the conclusion that it no longer was necessary for everyone to live in community sometime after 1994, those who wanted to do other things were more apt to be respected. Yet members expected that the decision to depart would be discussed with the Elders and not be made hastily. Then if people followed the proper channels, they would be helped to make the transition through the allocation of a portion of their salary toward a car and rent. Earlier, a lack of credit decreased the chances that a person would succeed apart from the group, but later it became possible to accumulate a credit history, which made the transition easier. Dick wanted to make sure I understood that they did not force people to stay:

> People, they come and stay for a time and say, "I think I probably got what I need, or I don't see it just this way and I am leaving," and they go. It's really a personal thing. Anyone of us can wake up tomorrow and talk to the Elders and say, "Lis-

ten. I feel like I am supposed to do something else after twenty-six years." Everybody has that kind of freedom.

Coming "of age" and leaving the group

Some, but not all, of the children raised in the group left when they became eighteen. Many have returned. Most intended only to leave for a few years. They usually felt their parents exaggerated the problems they would find outside of the community. A few were sure they would never return. Marie said that these were often children whose parents were unsure about their own commitment, making their children uncomfortable as well. Usually they were not allowed to leave until they were eighteen. They were not expected to simply go off on their own, but to either enter the military or live with relatives. Occasionally, when a child visited relatives outside the community, he or she was pressured to reject the group. The parents would then be expected to stop such visits, unless the outsider was another parent.

It was considered normal rebellious behavior for teenagers to want to leave the group, but it was hoped that by the time they reached eighteen, they would decide to commit themselves to it. In the late 1980s, life was particularly hard for the teenagers who expressed considerable dissatisfaction. While those before them had the benefit of an influx of many new members, newcomers had tapered off. The rural environment and the community's separation from everyone created a sense of isolation. One teenager declared that no one could imagine what it is like to graduate in a class of two, have no girls to date, have no privacy, and be totally isolated from everything. Many left as soon as they could. Chuck noted how the community dealt with this rejection:

> A lot of the kids that graduated decided that they wanted to go out and try to make a life out in the world as far as going somewhere different and doing something different. They're still in contact with us. I see them when they come up. They're like I'd say my nephews and nieces. They're out there experiencing and most of them think when they're done experiencing that they're going to come home and make this their life.

Those who were teenagers during my visit in 1994 exhibited far less dissatisfaction. One reason was their parents' renewed relationship with the Body. There was a steady influx of newcomers and visitors, and efforts were made to take young people on trips to the other communities.

Those who had been raised in the group and left but then returned were fairly consistent in their descriptions of why they came home. They usually agreed that loneliness was the key problem. They missed the accustomed communication or approval and found that outsiders did not accept their honesty. Parents were invariably thrilled when their children returned. A man told me he hoped his sons were ill-equipped to live on the outside. He believed that if they felt different from other people, they would always return.

It was clear that accepting the core beliefs of the group and living outside of it did not coincide. Members felt it was difficult to continue to believe in the calling to serve God as a group when forced to become concerned with individual survival. After someone left, he or she always felt guilty about not being available for when the time came to fulfill this calling. Yet it was also difficult to return, because people felt like failures. In addition, because leaving is considered evidence of disloyalty, the returnee must regain lost trust and status.

On rare occasions people were asked to leave. When members opened the community to those with different levels of commitment, they also became more selective about whom they accepted. Space in the group became limited because of the influx of families from the other communities. Resources were also limited, because many of these families had emotional problems and were unable to contribute a great deal to the community. In addition, members received their energy from each other, and depressed people diminished it by undermining what was being done. The departure of these individuals was often followed by what was described as a "release of tension." Anita outlined what would happen when someone steadfastly refused to contribute to the community:

> We'd get them some kind of counseling to figure out their part and where they can contribute. If they are setting us back and

> not working, not contributing, not participating, they do not get kicked out. There is usually a talking confrontation about it, and then the decision is made. Perhaps they need to leave.

She remembered someone who was asked to leave: "He was just very unhappy and women did not feel very secure around him and stuff. So I think he basically wanted to leave more than he had to." Dick gave further insight into what might cause someone to be asked to leave:

> They start doing different things and maybe won't comply with the things they wanted to do. We would say to that person, "Do you want to do this or do something else?" If they don't look like they want to turn around—drinking, smoking, and whatever—we would ask them probably to leave. It's not as though we are going to observe that you are doing exactly this and exactly that in the space of one year, and then we will let you be. . . . it's not that tight at all. It's really by the "spirit" that God shows us about each person. It's pretty much done on that basis. We don't have to ask a lot of people to leave because people come and this is really what they are doing. I mean there are a lot more places an awful lot more fun. We work long hours and are gone most of the time. If you are not really wanting to work that hard because you don't have the vision of what it's all about, you may very well want to do something else with your life.

Conclusion

At one level it is apparent that ISOT is a successful commune because it provides its members with a sense of meaning and a way to order that meaning. They come together because of shared beliefs offering prescriptions for social interaction that help to establish a shared identity. They then structure their community accordingly, separating themselves from the wider community. But a shared identity is not an adequate explanation for the level of commitment it takes to sustain a community for any length of time.

Victor Turner's formulation provides a deeper understanding of the processes that ensure this level of commitment. The members of the ISOT community intentionally create and maintain certain social conditions that are amenable to a continuation of communitas values, even while playing increasingly structured roles. Through the manipulation of symbols of liminality during secular and sacred ritual they counteract threats to their level of commitment to the group. They continually remind each other to transcend mundane affairs and remember their lifelong commitment to an ultimate objective provided by a higher authority. In this way, communitas is nourished because liminal processes are integrated into the total social process.

Notes

1. A number of people and organizations have contributed to this study. I would especially like to thank the members of ISOT for all of the work they have done to help me understand their life in community. Robert Winzeler, professor at the University of Nevada, guided me through the study. Support was provided by a dissertation research grant from the National Science Foundation, the Society for the Scientific Study of Religion, and a Weyher Summer Grant from Westminster College of Salt Lake City.

2. I have known the members of ISOT since the early 1980s. A detailed account of their community can be found in my Ph.D. dissertation. It was completed in 1992 after an extended period of ethnographic research. I periodically returned to visit through 1994.

3. More detailed information about these beliefs can be found in Marie's pamphlets that are published by the community. A few have been included in references cited.

4. I was told by this state employee that a new government policy in California was to abolish Group Homes and send children directly to Juvenile Hall. He had hired this man, who had closed down other Group Homes, to investigate the commune covertly by expressing his intentions to join the community. I was researching ISOT at the time, and, like the members of ISOT, did not suspect the intentions of this individual.

5. Narratives in this chapter were provided by randomly selected members of ISOT in 1994. They are edited only for clarity. Other paraphrased conversations came from prior visits.

Reference List

Burgess, Stanley M., and Gary B. McGee, eds. 1988. *Dictionary of Pentecostal and Charismatic Movements.* Grand Rapids, Mich.: Zondervan.

Moore, Sally F., and Barbara G. Myerhoff, eds. 1977. *Secular Ritual.* Assen, The Netherlands: Van Gorcum.

Siegler, Gretchen. 1992. The Structure of Antistructure: The Development Organization of a Religious Community in a Small Western Town. Ph.D. diss., University of Nevada at Reno.

Tolbert, E. Marie [E. Marie White]. 1970. *Responsibility in Eldership.* Alturas, Calif.: ISOT Press.

———. 1974. *Cursed or Blessed, the Dichotomy of Man.* Alturas, Calif.: ISOT Press.

———. 1976. *Articles of Faith.* Canby, Calif.: ISOT Press.

———. 1979. *A Family Called ISOT.* Canby, Calif.: ISOT Press.

———. 1982. *The Prophets Foretell.* Canby, Calif.: ISOT Press.

———. 1988. *New Covenant Celebrations.* Canby, Calif.: ISOT Press.

———. 1990. *The Symbols of Our Faith.* Canby, Calif.: ISOT Press.

Turner, Victor. 1969. *The Ritual Process: Structure and Anti-Structure.* Chicago: Aldine.

———. 1974. Liminal to Liminoid, in Play, Flow, and Ritual: An Essay in Comparative Symbology. *Rice University Studies* 60, no. 3:53–92.

———. 1977. Variations on a Theme of Liminality. In *Secular Ritual,* edited by Sally F. Moore and Barbara G. Myerhoff, 36–54. Assen, The Netherlands: Van Gorcum.

Turner, Victor, ed. 1982. *Celebration: Studies in Festivity and Ritual.* Washington, D.C.: Smithsonian Institution Press.

Turner, Victor, and Edith Turner. 1978. *Image and Pilgrimage in Christian Culture: Anthropological Perspectives.* Oxford: Blackwell.

Van Gennep, Arnold. 1960. *The Rites of Passage.* Translated by Monika B. Vizedom and Gabrielle L. Caffee. Chicago: University of Chicago Press.

Weber, Max. 1968. *On Charisma and Institution Building.* Edited by S. N. Eisenstadt. Chicago: University of Chicago Press.

4

Between Two Worlds: Community, Liminality, and the Development of Alternative Marriage Systems

Lawrence Foster

During the turbulent period of expansion and ferment of the 1830s and 1840s when Jacksonian Americans were becoming involved in an extraordinary variety of new religious and social movements, thousands of New Englanders and transplanted New Englanders joined communal religious groups that rejected existing marriage and nuclear family patterns. Instead, such groups organized new communities around alternative family or sex-role models as divergent as the celibacy of the Shakers, the complex marriage of the Oneida Community, and the polygamy of the Mormons. Historians and popular writers generally have caricatured or patronized these ventures. The communities founded by these groups are said inevitably to have "failed" because they were out of touch with the developing economic and industrial order, or because their leaders and members were unstable and psychologically maladjusted, or because they did not fit into the larger American "consensus," whatever that may have been (Bestor 1970, 289–94).

Such approaches fail to explain how functioning systems of celibacy, group marriage, and polygamy could have developed and attracted so many nineteenth-century descendants of the New England

Puritans. How were such alternative family systems conceived, introduced, and institutionalized—lasting for more than a quarter of a century in each case? What were these communal groups trying to accomplish, and how successful were they in terms of their own objectives and the new worldviews they were attempting to develop?

To begin to answer such questions, I immersed myself in the primary manuscript and printed holdings for each group, attempting to recapture at the deepest possible emotional level what it must have been like to be an early Shaker, Oneidan, or Mormon. This effort inevitably led me toward anthropological perspectives. Particularly valuable was the work on problems of acculturation that was implicit or explicit in the studies of millennial and ecstatic religious movements by anthropologists such as Anthony F. C. Wallace (1956), Kenelm Burridge (1969), Victor Turner (1969), I. M. Lewis (1971), and others. I became convinced that millennial movements were part of a complex attempt to create the intellectual and social synthesis for a new society—in their terms, "a new heaven and a new earth."

During periods of extensive cultural interaction and perceived social crisis, individuals and groups characteristically try to return to their cultural roots and reinterpret old values in a new social context. These millennial communitarians thus could be viewed as part of a self-conscious attempt to create a sort of Anglo-American ethnicity. Their ventures were analogous in many respects to the efforts of non-WASP immigrant groups to revive their own national roots, to develop or recapture a sense of distinctively Greek, Irish, Polish, or other national identity. Like Perry Miller's Puritans, these Yankee communitarians provide "an ideal laboratory" through which the actual process of social change can be illustrated at both the individual and group levels (Miller 1961, foreword). The specific marital solutions these antebellum communitarians developed may have been idiosyncratic; the issues of social organization with which they struggled, however, are centrally important for understanding changes in the family and larger nineteenth-century American social stresses.

One of the most difficult problems posed by these communitarian ventures was the process by which the transition to new marital and religious forms occurred. Although the functioning communities that marked the end product of each transition were internally consistent for the most part, both intellectually and socially, the actual transition from monogamy to alternative family systems appeared initially to lack any discernible order. For instance, during the early Shaker transition to a form of celibate communal organization between 1785 and 1797, they engaged in many extreme revivalistic activities. These not only included noisy services with singing, shouting, and dancing that could be heard from more than two miles away, but also occasional trances, flagellation, and even dancing naked. Though considerably more restrained, Mormon activities during their transition to a functioning polygamous system between 1841 and 1847 also were marked by numerous excesses. Perhaps the most intellectually puzzling actions were those of the prophet Joseph Smith himself, who, according to internal Mormon sources, took as wives in a full physical sense women who were already legally married to other men. And during the peak period of internal and external tension in the Oneida Community during the early 1850s, an extraordinary range of emotional problems developed. These tensions culminated in the course of one six-month period between March and August 1852, when the community announced its temporary discontinuance of complex marriage in order to devote its efforts to "the abolition of death."

Such severe internal conflicts and strange external manifestations could be seen as simply an inevitable byproduct of any attempt to lead an entire group of people to adopt new marital forms that were radically at variance with their earlier belief and practice. But were these external disorders simply "sound and fury, signifying nothing," or did such experiences have some meaning and value in themselves that was not immediately obvious to the outside observer? Was there a deeper order underlying the apparent surface confusion of these transition periods?

The work of Victor Turner, particularly *The Ritual Process: Structure and Anti-Structure* (1969), opened a wider perspective on both the external structural characteristics and the internal emotional significance of such social transitions. Turner began with Arnold Van Gennep's analysis of ritual "rites of passage" or transition, which are marked by three phases: first, a separation, disaggregation, or breakdown of an old status or order; second, an intermediary or "liminal" period when neither the old nor the new standards are in effect: and third, a reaggregation or establishment of a new order (Van Gennep 1960)

Turner's most provocative insights are found in his analysis of the dynamics of the liminal or transition period between two opposing or partially contradictory states of being, whether as part of individual rites of passage or of larger social transitions. During such a period, a person's status is ambiguous; he or she is caught "betwixt and between the positions assigned and arrayed by law, custom, convention, and ceremonial" (Turner 1969, 81). Frequently initiates are represented as possessing nothing, and are expected to obey their instructors completely and accept arbitrary punishment or seemingly irrational demands without complaint. "It is as though they are being reduced or ground down to a uniform condition to be fashioned anew and endowed with additional powers to enable them to cope with their new station in life" (Turner 1969, 81).

Accompanying the temporary ceremonial breakdown of normal secular distinctions of rank, status, and obligation in the liminal period is an intense egalitarianism and sense of emotional unity. There is an overriding feeling of direct personal communion, a blend "of lowliness and sacredness, of homogeneity and comradeship."

> It is as though there are here two major "models" for human interrelatedness, juxtaposed and alternating. The first is of society as a structured, differentiated, and often hierarchical system of politico-legal-economic positions with many types of evaluation, separating men in terms of "more" or "less." The second, which emerges recognizably in the liminal period, is of society as an unstructured or rudimentarily structured and relatively undifferentiated *comitatus*, or community, or even communion of equal individuals who submit together to the general authority of the ritual elders. (Turner 1969, 82)

Turner characterizes this latter state as one of "communitas." In a healthy society, he emphasizes, both "structure" as well as direct, experiential "anti-structure" or "communitas" are present in a creative, fluctuating tension.

With Victor Turner's insights in mind, many otherwise puzzling aspects of the experiences of these communal groups fell into place. It was exhilarating to discover that all three groups explicitly articulated their own process of transition in similar terms, and that those terms were wholly compatible with Turner's analysis as well. Although the specific *content* of the new order that each group was trying to achieve differed greatly, the *process*, issues, and personal experiences during the intermediary period transcended such surface differences. A special type of creativity, suffused with wonder, underlay the varied and seemingly bizarre external behaviors.

The Shaker transition to celibacy

The Shakers were particularly articulate in assessing the value and ambiguous potential of the "liminal" period, the tensions between structure and anti-structure. In discussing the formation of their Northeastern societies between 1785 and 1797, the formation of their Midwestern societies between 1807 and 1811, and the turbulent period of "spiritual manifestations" from 1837 to 1845, almost every early Shaker doctrinal and historical work self-consciously described and analyzed their experiences within a supernatural framework using categories virtually identical to those that Turner would later use from a secular perspective.

Every Shaker analysis began with their primary attempt to overcome the pull of their "fallen," "carnal" nature, to wholly separate themselves from an evil world and break down that old order within themselves as well. To this end they shook, sang, shouted, and often danced all night until literal exhaustion. Reliable accounts by ex-Shakers such as the one by Thomas Brown (1812) further indicate that in more extreme instances Believers would lay themselves down upon chains, sticks, and ropes in every humiliating and mortifying posture imaginable. In a few exceptional instances of self-negation, they would even strip and dance naked to kill their pride (Foster 1981, 41–43).

The first Shaker doctrinal account admits that to the uninvolved outsider, such activities appeared "like the most unaccountable confusion," yet to Believers it was "the gift and work of God"

([Young] 1810, xxxvi). The primary emotional tone in the various internal Shaker records, a tone that almost overpowers the reader at times, is the extraordinary love, comradeship, and closeness that Believers felt for each other. So deep was this sense of communion that Believers became convinced that Ann Lee, their leader, literally embodied the spirit of God in their midst.

The many extreme manifestations may well have been an inevitable concomitant of the breakdown of the old order and the transition to new forms, but more mature Believers such as Joseph Meacham and Lucy Wright sought as soon as possible to lead the Society into a new order. During the transition phase when neither the old order nor the as-yet-unborn new state could be the basis of authority, the extraordinary manifestations had been essential. As the so-called secret book of the Elders noted, in a passage suggesting an almost secular awareness of the function and origins of such phenomena:

> Divine miracles have generally attended the ushering in of new and extraordinary dispensations of God to a dark and benighted world; because they carry to the minds of the lost children of men, the strongest evidence of the sacred messenger's divine authority. But when that divine authority is once established in the hearts of honest believers, a continuance of outward miracles, for that purpose, is no longer necessary. ([Bishop and Wells] 1816, 254)

Looking back, another Shaker account described the overall process of transformation, emphasizing the necessary functions of both structure and antistructure. The first leaders of the Society were compared to "people going into a new country, and settling in the wilderness, where the first object is to cut and clear the land, and burn the rubbish, before the ground can be suitably prepared for cultivation." This process is accompanied by vigorous activity, by much noise, bustle, and confusion. "But when the land is sufficiently cleared, and the rubbish consumed, and the wild vermin have all retreated, and the careful husbandman has securely fenced his field, he can go on to prepare and cultivate his ground in peace" ([Green and Wells] 1823, xii).

Throughout Shaker history during times of crisis and revival, ecstatic phenomena would return with renewed force as individuals and the group as a whole sought to find ultimate sanction for a religious and social way of life that was being called into question. Shaker success before the Civil War can be attributed in large part to their ability to achieve an effective balance between the concern for individual creativity and self-expression and the necessary constraints of their functioning communal order, between the dialectical tensions of structure and anti-structure.

The Mormon transition to polygamy

Equally complex and suggestive in terms of Turner's theories of liminality and communitas are some of the irregularities and forgotten practices associated with Joseph Smith's introduction of a form of polygamy among his closest associates in Nauvoo, Illinois, during the early 1840s. Perhaps most difficult to interpret is the evidence that Joseph asked some of his closest associates to give their wives to him and that he may have sustained full sexual relations with some women who were at the same time legally the wives of other men (Foster 1981, 159–60).

Non-Mormons have typically assumed that Smith was simply indulging his sexual impulses in such cases. In fact, the process was considerably more complex than such a "commonsense" point of view recognizes. It is best understood in the context of the problems inherent in any transitional period between two different and partially incompatible value systems of the type Turner analyzes.

Joseph Smith's 1843 revelation on plural and celestial marriage makes clear that conventional marriages based on the standards of the external world were not considered valid for eternity. The revelation states: "All covenants, contracts, bonds, obligations, oaths, vows, performances, connections, associations, or expectations, that are not made and entered into, and sealed, by the Holy Spirit of promise, of him who is anointed, both as well for time and for all eternity . . . are of no efficacy, virtue, or force in and after the resurrection from the dead" (*Deseret News Extra*, 14 September 1852, cited in full in Foster 1981, 249–55)

Later Mormon theology has taken this statement as referring

to the afterlife; however, in the millenarian context of Nauvoo and early Utah, Mormon leaders attempted to apply presumptive heavenly standards directly on earth. Earthly and heavenly standards were seen as inextricably intertwined; an imminent earthly millennium was to be realized. This meant that existing marriage standards were invalid and that the only valid marriages were those sanctioned under the "new and everlasting covenant" as sealed and practiced on earth. Mormon initiatory ceremonies, from baptism to the more elaborate temple rites, involved a rebirth into a new and different world that was in the process of being created on earth by the church. Prior to the initiation into the new standards, however, there was a brief but disruptive interregnum when neither set of standards was operative and the basis of social authority was unclear.

A former member of Smith's secret Council of Fifty, which helped to regulate this transition, recalled:

> About the same time [1842] the doctrine of "sealing" for an eternal state was introduced, and the Saints were given to understand that their marriage relations with each other were not valid. . . . That they were married to each other only by their own covenants, and that if their marriage relations had not been productive of blessings and peace, and they felt it oppressive to remain together, they were at liberty to make their own choice, as much as if they had not been married. That it was a sin for people to live together, and raise or beget children, in alienation from each other. (Lee 1877, 146–47)

In addition to this larger argument that the revelation on plural and celestial marriage superseded all earthly bonds and covenants, a second argument also suggests why Joseph Smith might have asked for the wives of other men. In a public speech on 8 October 1861, Brigham Young discussed the ways "in which a woman might leave a man lawfully." The primary valid cause for a divorce was: "When a woman becomes alienated in her feelings & affections from her husband." In addition, "if the woman Preferred—another man higher in authority & he is willing to take her & her husband gives her up—there is no Bill of divorce required . . ." (Beck 1859–65).

Such a practice of "moving up" in the hierarchy without a formal divorce may well have originated with Joseph Smith.

There is a third, more speculative explanation that could further help account for cases in which Joseph Smith appears to have approached or taken married women as plural wives. According to a number of sources, including an internal Mormon statement, it may have been possible in some cases for a proxy husband to be assigned by the president of the Mormon Church, through the power of the holy anointing, to serve the part of a temporary husband for wives of men absent on long missionary assignments. The children born under such arrangements could be viewed as belonging to the first man, who was considered in some sense to have been temporarily "dead." Thus, while a man was absent in the service of his church, his "kingdom," which was heavily dependent on the number of his children, would not suffer loss. If such an extraordinary millenarian variation on the Hebrew practice of the levirate ever existed, it was only practiced on a very limited scale in the emotionally superheated fervor of the transition from the old order to the new (Foster 1981, 163–66).

How is one to understand the significance of the many extraordinary activities associated with the introduction of Mormon polygamy in the 1840s? Although many of the phenomena might initially appear to be due simply to emotional excess, Turner's analysis of the liminal phase of rites of passage suggests a broader perspective. During the Mormon liminal period, there was both a sense of passionate involvement, camaraderie, and enthusiasm of selfless Mormon dedication to achieving the supremely important goal of realizing the kingdom of heaven on earth, and a willingness, as in the ritual process, to follow trusted leaders implicitly in doing whatever they might demand.

Distinctions between "mine" and "thine" were reduced to an absolute minimum in the face of a common challenge and crisis. In the oft-repeated phrase of Smith's close associate Heber C. Kimball, Mormons undergoing this transition process were expected to become as "clay in the hands of the potter"; totally subordinating their wills to that of the group, they would allow themselves to be reshaped into a new and more perfect social form as Latter-day Saints (Foster 1987, 131–52).

This intense camaraderie combined with total loyalty to leaders is clearly indicated in Joseph Smith's letter proposing marriage to Nancy Rigdon, daughter of one of his closest associates. The letter asserts that "Happiness is the object and design of our existence" but that this can only be achieved through "virtue, uprightness, faithfulness, holiness and keeping all the commandments of God."

> But we cannot keep all the commandments without first knowing them. That which is wrong under one circumstance, may be, and often is, right under another. A parent may whip a child, and justly too, because he stole an apple; whereas if the child had asked for the apple, and the parent had given it, the child would have eaten it with a better appetite. . . . all things shall be made known unto them in mine own due time, and in the end they shall have joy. (Smith 1948, 5:136)

The potential disruptiveness of such an approach when seen from the context of conventional social standards is easy to understand. Smith's passionate emotional engagement with his followers was a two-edged sword that could lead either to passionate love or, equally, to passionate hatred. There seemed to be no middle ground. Either one was totally for the prophet or one was totally against him. Only after Smith's assassination in 1844 and the migration of a majority of his followers to the isolated Great Basin region in 1847 were Brigham Young and his associates able eventually to regularize and control the forces that Joseph Smith's extraordinary personality had projected onto the world of his Latter-day Saints.

The Oneida transition to complex marriage

Efforts by the Oneida Community to introduce its extraordinary form of "complex" or group marriage in the late 1840s and early 1850s are also strongly suggestive in terms of Turner's theories of ritual process and liminality. John Humphrey Noyes, founder and key leader of the group throughout its existence from 1848 to 1881, was a Yale-trained academic who used his acute and idiosyncratic mind to reflect on his goals and attempt to implement them in his remarkable communal experiment at Oneida. Unlike the celibacy of the Shakers, which did away with direct sexual relations, or the polygamy of Mormons, which expanded a form of patriarchal family organization, Noyes's complex marriage attempted to institutionalize what might be seen as a permanent state of liminality in which heterosexual barriers among adults in his "enlarged family" were removed throughout a more than thirty-year period.

As described in his "Bible Argument" manifesto written in 1848, John Humphrey Noyes's chief goal in reorganizing relations between the sexes was to break down the earthly institution of marriage, "which assigns the exclusive possession of one woman to one man," and, instead, to enlarge and refocus sexual as well as other loyalties to the level of the entire community. The "I-spirit" would be replaced with the "We-spirit," resulting in a perfect unity of interest like that of the Day of Pentecost, in which all would be one, even as the Father is one (Oneida Association 1849, 18–42).

As eventually set up at Oneida, all members lived together in one large communal Mansion House, ate together, worked together, had a system of communal child rearing, and shared all but the most basic property in common. Adult men and women considered themselves married to the group in a "complex marriage" in which love, including heterosexual intercourse among adults, could be expressed freely within the entire community. At the same time, the community rigorously broke up all exclusive romantic attachments (which were described as "special love," an antisocial behavior threatening communal order) and stressed absolute loyalty to John Humphrey Noyes's religious principles and leadership.

The process by which this extraordinary system was set up during the first five years of the Oneida Community's existence after 1848 was, not surprisingly, characterized by remarkable turbulence. On the one hand, there was a powerful sense of closeness, communion, and comradeship associated with the breakdown of individual sexual and emotional exclusivity as the group attempted to realize the kingdom of heaven on earth. On the other hand, the community newspapers during those years stressed unquestioning obedience, unity, love, harmony, right devotion, and the like, suggesting the extent to which such qualities were seen as absent at the time. Psychosomatic illnesses and faith cures were frequently discussed, and several cases of temporary insanity and suicidal tendencies were mentioned. External pressures, due in part to disgruntled former members, also created problems for the community.

The peak of these difficulties and the beginning of their resolution apparently came between March and August 1852. In response to an all-out newspaper crusade against the community, the *Oneida Circular* on 7 March 1852 announced that despite the community's continuing commitment to its complex marriage system, it was temporarily discontinuing the practice until public feeling abated. By this action, the community declared, it was graphically demonstrating that it was "not attached to forms," even its own. "To be able to conform to *any* circumstances, and *any* institutions, and still preserve spiritual freedom" was the goal of the perfectionists. The community's new efforts would be devoted to publicizing its ideas through its newspaper and to what must appear a most puzzling objective indeed—the "abolition of death."

The details of what was going on during this period are discussed elsewhere (Foster 1991, 103–20) and can only be summarized here. When the community spoke about the abolition of "disease and death," it was using an internal code to refer to the community's severe mental and emotional problems (many of them associated with the introduction of complex marriage). Numerous articles focused on topics such as nervousness, faith and unbelief, insanity, spiritualist excesses, inattention, the uselessness of self-condemnation, problems of insubordination, and the like. Threats of internal apostasy, and the problems of "bridling sensuality," and how to place such drives at the service of the larger community were also emphasized. In essence, the Oneida Community was deliberately retrenching, performing an internal and external penance that would prepare a solid foundation for a second and successful effort to reintroduce complex marriage in August 1852.

The communal system that fully emerged by the mid-1850s and was successfully maintained for the next quarter century was one of the most radical communal efforts to break down conventional sex-role patterns and barriers between individuals in America (Foster 1991, 91–102). As late as 1875, just five years before the breakup of the Oneida Community, the journalist Charles Nordhoff noted Oneida's extraordinary flexibility in everything from work assignments to recreation to meal schedules, and its strong desire to avoid getting locked into routines (Nordhoff 1875, 286). Yet counterposed to such "anti-structure" was the absolute commitment of the group to the leadership of John Humphrey Noyes and to a series of complex control mechanisms, including daily religious-and-business meetings that all adults attended, an informal method of group feedback and control called "mutual criticism," and a difficult voluntary method of birth control by *coitus reservatus* known as "male continence."

Throughout the entire process of transition to complex marriage, and indeed until the final breakup of the community in 1881, John Humphrey Noyes reflected eloquently on the transitional problems of social order and disorder that Turner would refer to as "structure" and "anti-structure." Noyes sought always to maintain a harmonious balance between what he called "the two great principles of human existence," "solidarity" and "liberty," which, though they might appear antithetical, "like the centripetal and centrifugal forces of Nature," were in fact "designed to act upon human life in equilibrium" (*Circular*, 4 January 1852). While lyrically celebrating the profound emotional power of love in its many forms, Noyes also successfully set in place structures to contain the potential excesses of such compelling yet problematic emotional states.

Understanding communal transitions

What are the implications of the work of anthropologists such as Victor Turner for the relationship of anthropology and history, especially in studies of the transition process in close-knit communal groups? As indicated above, Turner's theories can sensitize us to the general patterns of development of such groups and help us to be more aware of how they understood their own transition experiences, particularly the complex interplay between individual and communal concerns. Yet the chief value of Turner's work lies not so much in any specific theories, as in his ability to exemplify in his own studies the creative tension between structure and antistructure.

As any good historian should do, Turner began with the raw material of experience. Whether he was conducting fieldwork or engaging in historical scholarship, he attempted to take seriously the values and concerns of his native informants and to use his materials to generate his analytical categories rather than attempting to impose external models that did not really fit his materials. But Turner did not stop with isolated fieldwork or case studies, as so many historians and other scholars are wont to do. Instead, he sought to discover larger regularities in human experience that go beyond particular time and culture-bound contexts. The result is a special sort of creative synthesis, which maintains a balance between both structure and antistructure.

Such an approach should serve as a model for other historians. Every good historian can be viewed in some sense as an anthropologist of the past. In L. P. Hartley's words: "The past is a foreign country; they do things differently there" (1954, 1). The historian's task is to understand the different ways of looking at and living in the world in different times and places, and to translate such experiences into the present so that they have meaning for our own time as well. This is a process of comprehension undergone by the religious prophet or by any creative figure, who enters the vault of experience and then returns to the everyday world to attempt to translate that deeper experience into terms that can be understood by the layperson. Like the anthropologist, prophet, or creative individual, the historian ultimately will be unsuccessful in recapturing the full richness of human experience. But there is, I am convinced, continuing value in the pursuit of an impossible ideal.

Reference List

Beck, James. 1859–65. Notebook I. In Archives of the Church of Jesus Christ of Latter-day Saints, Salt Lake City, Utah.

Bestor, Arthur E. 1970. *Backwoods Utopias: The Sectarian and Owenite Phase of Communitarian Socialism in America, 1663–1829*. 2d enl. ed. Philadelphia: University of Pennsylvania Press.

[Bishop, Rufus, and Seth Y. Wells, eds.] 1816. *Testimonies of the Life, Character, Revelations, and Doctrines of Our Ever Blessed Mother Ann Lee, and the Elders with Her*. Hancock, Mass.: J. Tallcott & J. Deming, Junrs.

Brown, Thomas. 1812. *An Account of the People Called Shakers: Their Faith, Doctrine, and Practice*. Troy, N.Y.: Parker & Bliss.

Burridge, Kenelm. 1969. *New Heaven, New Earth: A Study of Millenarian Activities*. New York: Schocken.

Foster, Lawrence. 1981. *Religion and Sexuality: Three American Communal Experiments of the Nineteenth Century*. New York: Oxford University Press.

———. 1987. "Reluctant Polygamists": The Strains and Challenges of the Transition to Polygamy in a Prominent Mormon Family. In *Religion and Society in the American West: Historical Essays,* edited by Carl Guarneri and David Alvarez, 131–52. Lanham, Md.: University Press of America.

———. 1991. *Women, Family, and Utopia: Communal Experiments of the Shakers, the Oneida Community, and the Mormons*. Syracuse, N.Y.: Syracuse University Press.

[Green, Calvin, and Seth Y. Wells.] 1823. *A Summary View of the Millennial Church or United Society of Believers (Commonly Called Shakers)*. Albany, N.Y.: Packard & Van Benthuysen.

Hartley, L. P. 1954. *The Go-Between*. New York: Knopf.

Lee, John D. 1877. *Mormonism Unveiled; Including the Remarkable Life and Confessions of the Late Mormon Bishop, John D. Lee*. Edited by W. W. Bishop. St. Louis, Mo.: Bryan, Brand.

Lewis, I. M. 1971. *Ecstatic Religion: An Anthropological Study of Spirit Possession and Shamanism*. Baltimore: Penguin.

Miller, Perry. 1961. *The New England Mind: From Colony to Province*. Boston: Beacon.

Nordhoff, Charles. 1875. *The Communistic Societies of the United States: From Personal Visit and Observation*. New York: Harper.

Oneida Association. 1849. *First Annual Report of the Oneida Association*. Oneida Reserve, N.Y.: Leonard.

Smith, Joseph. 1948. *History of the Church of Jesus Christ of Latter-day Saints: Period I*. Edited by Brigham H. Roberts. 2d ed. rev. 6 vols. Salt Lake City, Utah: Deseret Book Company.

Turner, Victor. 1969. *The Ritual Process: Structure and Anti-Structure*. Chicago: Aldine.

Van Gennep, Arnold. 1960. *The Rites of Passage*. Translated by Monika B. Vizedom and Gabrielle L. Caffee. Chicago: University of Chicago Press.

Wallace, Anthony F. C. 1956. Revitalization Movements. *American Anthropologist* 58:264–81.

[Young, Benjamin S.] 1810. *The Testimony of Christ's Second Appearing; Containing a General Statement of All Things Pertaining to the Faith and Practice of the Church of God in This Latter Day*. 2d ed. Albany, N.Y.: E. & E. Hosford.

5

The Borderlands of Community: Refugee Camps, Intentional Communities, and Liminality

Matthew Renfro-Sargent

People are constantly in motion, and the boundaries of societies are fluid. A confluence of factors propels people voluntarily and involuntarily into new destinations. This paper focuses on two kinds of groups: voluntary groups, made up of individuals who decide to convert to a communal way of living, and involuntary groups, made up of individuals who are compelled by global, regional, or geopolitical factors into becoming refugees. By joining a communal society and by relocating from one's native land to a refugee camp, an individual steps into a borderland—"a vague and undetermined place created by the emotional residue of an unnatural boundary" (Anzaldua 1987, 3). People in both kinds of groups struggle with identity and become dislocated within space and time—they enter a state of liminality.

This paper compares these vastly different experiences and suggests that both experiences constitute a state of liminality—an interim state between what has been and what will be in which individuals either struggle with their identities or with the distinction between *us* and *them*. Borderlands are places of transition. Those entering communal societies and those who are refugees have both moved away from a preexisting state of conflict. Here I compare members of Oneida, Brook Farm, and Hopedale communities with refugees among the Hmong, Palestinians, and Maya. Using the theoretical frames of Van Gennep's *Rites of Passage* (1960) and Victor Turner's elaboration of this work (1964), I explore the cultural ambiguities of the struggle with identity as people in both kinds of space become inhabitants of the borderlands of community.

Separation: The Movement Away from a State of Conflict

> The first phase of separation comprises symbolic behavior signifying the detachment of the individual or group either from an earlier fixed point in the social structures or a set of cultural conditions. . . .
>
> —Victor Turner

Groups move into a liminal state by moving away from a preexisting area of conflict. In the case of refugees, this movement is usually a survival response necessitated by conditions in their homelands. The Hmong, the Maya, and the Palestinians, peoples in three different parts of the world, faced such situations.

Hmong refugees moved due to Vietnam expansionism into Laos and Cambodia. The Hmong, it is argued, originated in the "steppes of Tibet, Mongolia, and old China" (Walker-Moffat 1995, 36). Throughout years of migration, the Hmong have located themselves throughout the Guizhou, Yunnan, Hunan, and Guangxi regions of southern China, northern parts of Vietnam, Laos, and Thailand. The mid-twentieth century brought the "superpower" nations to Southeast Asia. In the late sixties, the Lao Hmong found themselves recruited by the CIA to fight against the Pathet Lao, the Soviet Union–backed military regime (Long 1993; Zolberg, Suhrke, and Aguayo 1989). The Paris Agreement of 1973 forced the withdrawal of the United States from Vietnam. Wendy Walker-Moffat comments that the withdrawal of U.S. troops "also meant the withdrawal of U.S. military support for the Hmong army in Laos under General Vang Pao, the Lao Army, and the government of Lon Nol in Cambodia" (1995, 30).

With the U.S. departure, North Vietnam took control over South Vietnam, the Pathet Lao took power over Laos, and Cambodia became dominated by the Khmer Rouge, which also found support from the Soviet Union. During this time, notes Walker-Moffat, "more than two million people were displaced, and more than half of them eventually came to the United States as refugees" (1995, 30). However, as Aristide Zolberg and others point out, some of the Hmong stationed themselves at the border camps of Thailand and formed resistance groups against the new political regimes (1989, 168).

The turmoil in Southeast Asia continued well into the eighties, creating an unstable atmosphere between the above parties. In 1983–85 when the Vietnamese attacked Khmer border camps and pushed Cambodians and Laotians back into Thailand, they created thousands more refugees (Long 1993). Most of these refugees found themselves in the camps of Thailand, mainly in Ban Tong, Nam Yao, Sop Tuang, Ban Vinai, and Nong Khai (Hendricks and Downing 1986).

Likewise, the violent massacres of the Lucas Garcia regime and the Rios Montt government forced Maya refugees out of Guatemala in the 1980s (see Ferris 1987; Manz 1988). To understand the context in which these Guatemalans took flight, it is important to summarize historical events. In 1944, Juan Jose Arevalo was elected as president and "enacted agrarian reform legislation, labor and educational reforms, and an independent foreign policy line" (Ferris 1987, 25). Such a reform threatened the position of the dominant landed elite and also the United Fruit Company, which profited from the lands of Guatemala. In 1954, the CIA provided support for Col. Castillo Armas, who overthrew the Arbenz government. Since then, the military government has dominated the political spheres in Guatemala. According to Elizabeth Ferris, "massive U.S. military and economic aid in the 1960s provided support for an increasingly powerful military force" (1987, 25). Opposition leaders were continuously repressed by governmental death squads, which created an atmosphere in which insurgent guerrilla movements developed.

By 1982, the regime of General Efrain Rios Montt took control of the government. Through political and religious beliefs, Rios

Montt believed that it was "his duty to restore order and to triumph over the guerrilla forces" (Ferris 1987, 26–27). When the guerrilla organizations did not cooperate with Rios Montt, he not only attacked them but also violently attacked civilians who were thought to be supporters. The army was able to control the insurgent forces with violence and fear, but forced thousands to take flight, the majority being Maya peasants.

Turning to the Middle East, confrontations between Zionists and Palestinians in 1948 in Palestine sent Palestinians into bordering countries such as Lebanon, Syria, Jordan, and Egypt, while some remained on the West Bank and the Gaza Strip. The British occupation of 1918 to 1948 can be seen as the beginning of the demise of Palestine. The occupation not only brought the domination of colonialism but also an influx of Zionism. The majority of the Palestinian Arabs were rural peasants, while many of the British and Zionists enjoyed the privileges of elite status. Under British colonial rule Palestinians were subordinated within the political process, and it was the Palestinian Arab peasants who were the most threatened by the Zionist domination (Sayigh 1979, 6).

With the purchasing of land, according to Sayigh, and their boycott of Arab labor, the Zionists were able to "cut off alternative sources of income, whether in agriculture or industry" (1979, 25). This forced the *fellaheen* (peasants) into the marginal areas of land that were less fertile, and an adequate living off the land became more difficult to achieve. Colonial attitudes toward the Palestinian Arabs also reinforced their subordination. Sayigh summarizes these attitudes: "[T]he Palestinians do not exist; that they were only 'custodians' of the land, never its owners; that they formed a natural helot class for Israel's Spartans" (1979, 45).

The Zionists were able to use the British occupation to further an evolving Zionist state. On the one hand, by being seen as "elites" their dominant role was legitimized through British authority. This enabled them to "practice their performance, without having to face the heavy cost of controlling the indigenous population" (1979, 56). On the other hand, "through Britain's mediation, Jewish claims for compensation generated through persecution *in Europe* transformed into claims fixed upon *Palestine*, written into the [British] Mandate Protocol, legitimated at Versailles, and given substance through immigration" (1979, 56–57). Such a claim played upon the sympathies of international communities, while also legitimizing their goals of state formation. In 1948, the British announced that they would withdraw from Palestine on 15 May of that same year. Benjamin N. Schiff explains that the Zionists "seized the date, declaring independence the previous day" (1995, 14).

The population of the Arab exodus in 1948–49 numbered over 700,000. Palestinians numbering over 130,000 remained in what is now Israel, while 500,000 moved to the district of the West Bank and Gaza Strip (Zolberg, Suhrke, and Aguayo 1989, 240). Several factors described by Sayigh forced thousands of Palestinians into flight: "direct military attack on the villages; terrorism; lack of leadership; lack of arms; in short, chaos and fear" (1979, 64).

For refugees the process of separation marks the beginning of their struggle to retain, regain, or reinvent identity. The struggle is twofold. On the one hand, the refugee becomes a victim, and the loss of the homeland means the loss of autonomy and the beginning of dependency on others for survival. Julie Peteet describes the sentiments of many Palestinians during the early years as "a period of mourning." She notes, "The loss of land and the rupture of identities and social relations grounded in it was akin to the loss of a loved one" (1995b, 168). On the other hand, the refugees are seen by others as outsiders and people who are rootless. Lisa Malkki explains that the "refugees' loss of bodily connection to the national homelands came to be treated as *a loss of moral bearings.*" Thus, they were seen as "no longer trustworthy as 'honest citizens'" (1992, 32).

The uncertainty of identity under these conditions is exacerbated when refugees are considered unwelcome members of the host countries into which they flee. Duncan Earle describes how conflicts arose in Chiapas, Mexico, because some of the Mexicans felt that the Maya refugees would use "scarce community resources" or spread disease (1988, 264). According to Peteet, the Lebanese Maronites feared that the Palestinian refugees, who were largely Muslim, "would upset the sectarian balance and political status quo by serving as a focal point for the growing discontent of Lebanese Muslims and their eventual mobilization against Maronite domination" (1995b, 169).

While refugees are in the position of having been rejected by either their homelands or the lands into which they flee, people who join intentional communities have often rejected features of the mainstream society from which they turn. Although these people often feel as if they are "escaping" from conditions under which it is difficult to live, their movement away from society is voluntary. This difference is captured in Malkki's distinction between *uprooting* and *transplantation* (1992, 31–32). Uprooting occurs when "broken and dangling roots predominate—roots that threaten to wither, along with the ordinary loyalties of citizenship in a homeland" (1992, 32). Like a twister uprooting a tree, refugees have been uprooted from the land that provides them with sustenance and identity.

Those who choose to form intentional communities engage in transplantation, the moving of "live, viable roots." Malkki states,

> It strongly suggests . . . the colonial and postcolonial, usually privileged, category of "expatriates" who pick up their roots in an orderly manner from the "mother country," the originative culture-bed, and set about their "acclimatization" in the "foreign environment" or on "foreign soil" again, in an orderly manner. (1992, 31)

Although such an analogy does not perfectly depict the move to an intentional community in all its aspects, it does highlight the voluntary aspects of moving toward a communal lifestyle.

In other respects, however, the movement of individuals voluntarily into communal societies is similar to that of refugees in that the movement often arises from conflict. Robert Fogarty sees these communities as "sitting on that borderline between restoration and revolution" and "the waver between the pull of the past, the lure of the peaceful garden, and the promise of change and revolution" (1990, 176). Fogarty paints a picture of individuals who cannot survive any longer in their societies, so they feel they must either seek out the mythical utopian garden or react against their society with some form of revolution. To reach either goal, individuals must escape from their societies. This conflict with the mainstream society is a key element in the formation of almost all intentional communities.

To some individuals, mainstream society produces effects so harmful that they need to save themselves through exile. The explanation John Humphrey Noyes gave for constructing the Oneida community is illustrative: "The sin-system, the marriage-system, the work-system, and the death-system, are all one, and must be abolished together. Holiness, free-love, association in labor, and immortality constitute the chain of redemption and must come together in their true order" (Noyes cited in Fellman 1973, 49).

The formation of Brook Farm was influenced by the beliefs of a group of nineteenth-century transcendentalists who saw each individual as having a quasi-divine presence. This belief influenced a group of "well-educated, advantaged New Englanders" who felt that society was "a world dominated by sleazy politics, dead religions, sterile professions, and dollar-dominated businesses" (Spann 1989, 54–55). Edward K. Spann remarks that these individuals viewed the existence of this society to be at the expense of "those who were closest to life, farmers and workers, classes enslaved by their poverty to oppressively hard physical toil" (1989, 54–55).

George Ripley, who became highly swayed by these beliefs, established the Brook Farm cooperative. The construction of such a community was not only an escape from a devalued world but also a method for correcting it. Spann explains that Ripley was "convinced that the gap between intellectual and manual labor was the root of the social crisis" (1989, 56). He saw his community as the only way to eliminate class distinctions and to revitalize the individual and community. Labor and interaction within Brook Farm, in which everyone participated for the common good, were utilized to create a better environment than that of their previous one, which also remained a coexisting state outside the Farm.

Adin Ballou gives three reasons for the erection of the Hopedale community, all of which lead to negative connotations of his environment. His first reason was based on what he terms the *War System* (1972, 10–11). Ballou perceived this to be a type of boundary maintenance of society that uses "multiplex enginery of destruction" that crushes the "life of out of vast multitudes of people" (1972, 10). This *War System* was in direct opposition to the beliefs and zeal held by Ballou and his Christian followers, therefore forcing them to reject the system and its supporters. The *Politico-civil*

Government was Ballou's second reason for creating the Hopedale community. Here, Ballou paints a picture of an administration filled with corruption. This political system disregards the "requirements of the moral law and of the rights of the weak and defenseless" (1972, 11). Like Ripley, Ballou saw class difference as a social problem that needed to be abolished. He locates the root of class distinction in what he terms the *"spirit of competition, rivalry, self-aggrandizement, and open antagonism"* that dominated in the realm of capitalism (1972, 11–12; italics in the original). Such competition created the dichotomous dominant-subordinate relationship in society that, according to Ballou, engenders "discontent, ill-will, resentment, animosity, hatred, and sometimes the spirit of revenge and open violence" (1972, 12).

For Noyes, Ripley, and Ballou, it was industrialization leading to the increase in urbanization, the atomization of the individual, and the decrease in Christian values that manufactured an amoral society that had to be reformed. Under the realization that such a task was holistically impossible, these men, along with their followers, opted for alternative communities in which they could construct themselves.

During the process of separation people move away from their homelands or mainstream societies and toward a communal existence that provides protection for them. As Hostetler says, "Each communitarian society is attempting to create a small world of order and tranquility and, at the same time, to protect itself against intrusions from the outside world" (1974, 49). But before this world is reached, both refugees and communitarians must pass through the state of liminality.

Liminality: The sharing of identities

> [D]uring the intervening "liminal" period the state of the ritual subject is ambiguous, he passes through a realm which has few or none of the attributes of the past or coming state. . . .
>
> —Victor Turner

Borderlands extend far beyond physical boundaries—they can be found between sexes, generations, religions, and cultures. When refugees and community members move from one state of existence to another, they are moving their cultures. Their way of life begins to change with the first step, and with it their identity begins to shift, redefined by space and place. Old identities dissolve and new identities are formed in the borderlands, and this process of identity change can be sought after or forced upon those who enter the liminal state.

For both refugees and community members the place of origin was home and identity, which also represented independence and control. "A homeland has its landmark, which may be features of high visibility and public significance, such as monuments, shrines, a hallowed battlefield or cemetery." Further, "These visible signs serve to enhance a people's sense of identity," says Yi-fu Tuan (1977, 159). The individual's world, belief system, ideology, and values are all constructed through the intertwined places of their home. If these places are destroyed, says Tuan, the individuals become "demoralized, since the ruin of their settlement implies the ruin of their cosmos" (1977, 147). To be anchored to a place is to be secure. To move is to give up that security.

Borderlands constitute a world between worlds, so that wherever borderlands exist, there is a state of liminality. Refugee camps and intentional communities are worlds within worlds—spaces in which people live on their own but cannot survive without assistance from the outside. The anthropological significance of borderlands is that they represent the struggle for identity or distinction. They are places of transition in which identity is shared but problematic. There begins the process of restructuring identity. The refugee camp, disconnected from the homeland and reinforced by the closed doors of the host country, becomes the site of the refugees' forced marginality.

The struggle for identity is collective but varies according to factors such as age, sex, and experience. Hmong elders yearned for a return to a Laos with which they had identified for the majority of their lives. The middle generation of Hmong refugees, which had experienced much of the violence and atrocity of warfare, was split between fighting back through guerrilla movements and searching for a secure sanctuary. Children who were born in the camps, in contrast, sought resettlement in a new country, their identities linked only to the refugee camps themselves. Persuaded by stories told by their resettled relatives and friends, plus stories from aid workers in the camps, the camp children saw resettlement as the agency of escape toward a new and better life (Long 1993).

The struggle within refugee camps can come to represent the survival of a collective identity and nationality. The Palestinians redefined and reconfigured the villages of Palestine within their refugee camps. "Place, or village, in the Palestinian consciousness is what ties a person to the space of Palestine. Palestinians identify and refer to one another in terms of village or region of origin," notes Peteet (1995b, 170). This village identification reinforced solidarity and strength by recreating the image of the nation within the camps.

This use of remembered space can also be seen within the Maya refugee camps. The commonality of suffering and refugee status forced into being a community. Maya gained strength through the organization of camp social institutions, such as stores, schools, and medical centers to help the people as a whole. The Permanent Commission of Representatives of Guatemala's Refugees (CCPP) was formed with elected representatives from each camp. These representatives then met, giving voice to the people in the camps, especially in terms of repatriation (Peteet 1995a; U.S. Committee for Refugees 1995, 182).

For the refugee, the community of the camp comes before the individual self. Camps become a place of collective identity and communal existence, and this existence assures survival. Within each camp, each household, and each family, individuals are under the control of the rules that the host country or camp leaders create. This loss of power is a key factor in the loss of the old identity.

Rules, regulations, and restrictions within camps and communes often contribute to the loss of personal identity and often become an obstacle that refugees must surmount. The Hmong at the Ban Vinai camp, for example, were given numbers and were known to officials by these numbers, a process that can have a dehumanizing effect on the individual, although it was ostensibly adopted for the purpose of facilitating the registration of individuals with the United Nations High Commissioner of Refugees (UNHCR). Refugees also must obtain sponsors in a third country before they are allowed to resettle. This was difficult to accomplish and often led to unwanted repatriation for many among the Hmong.

The camps often resembled what Foucault referred to as "total institutions"—an arena in which the body is disciplined and control is built into the very structure itself and its daily routine. Like prisons, refugee camps are often surrounded by fences and armed guards, and are sometimes even run by members of correctional services. In a Hong Kong camp that housed Vietnamese refugees, camp officials built internal fences that prevented development of community and tended to break down relationships among individuals so that they would want to repatriate instead of staying within the camp (Peteet 1995a). In refugee camps in Thailand, the government "prohibited education past the sixth year" to deny refugees any incentive for staying in the camps rather than repatriating (Long 1993, 80).

These tactics were also used by Mexico, which housed the majority of the Maya refugees. After the violent counterinsurgency campaigns of the Guatemalan government, many of the indigenous population fled into neighboring Chiapas, Mexico, where sixty-nine camps have been recognized by the UNHCR, most of which were constructed near the border. From the initial border crossings, the Mexican authorities and their Commission to Assist Refugees (COMAR) have distanced themselves from the turmoil that the Guatemalan victims had escaped. First, at the time of the influx of Maya refugees, Mexico's policy for accepting political asylum seekers was limited. Jason Clay explains that a "well-founded fear of personal persecution or actual physical violence of a random nature does not qualify one for asylum" (1984a, 47). Because of this, Mexican authorities granted the refugees a ninety-day visa that restricted them to within fifty miles of the border. Officially, then, the refugees were viewed as being only "temporary visitors," which reinforced the uprootedness that began in Guatemala (1984a, 48).

Secondly, the Mexican authorities initiated a program in the mid-1980s that relocated the refugees away from the Chiapas/Guatemalan border. The political structure in Chiapas was highly volatile, with the indigenous population being the most impoverished in the state, both highly unemployed and underemployed. Clay described the Mexican government as having fear that the "aroused consciousness of Mayan Indians in Guatemala will infect the impoverished Mayans of Chiapas" (1984a, 48). The authorities also wanted to prevent any future attacks by the Guatemalan military, which crossed the border to violently murder the refugees. Their action, however, was based on the need to protect their own citizens from any possible crossfire.

Their relocation program did not consider the position of the Maya refugees. The Maya spoke little Spanish, the predominant language in Mexico. This inhibited interaction in other states (1984a, 48). Given the fact that Chiapas was also populated by Maya, the refugees were able to interact better with the inhabitants of Chiapas. This was important for those who attempted employment. Since there were also Maya in Chiapas, some of whom were relatives of the refugees, the Guatemalan refugees were able to maintain their identity. Finally, Chiapas is closer to Guatemala than the destination of the relocation program, Campeche. The majority of the refugees saw themselves repatriating to Guatemala once safety was assured. The Maya did not want to assimilate into the Mexican culture. They were Maya; more importantly, they were Guatemalan Maya.

The third method by which Mexican authorities attempted to distance themselves from the refugees was the construction of the camp itself. For example, the camp of La Gloria de San Caralampio was surrounded by barbed wire (Manz 1984, 52). This created the same atmosphere as the Vietnamese camps mentioned above. Beatrice Manz described how "2,800 residents are living under sheets of nylon, in part, it seems, because COMAR will not allow them to construct permanent structures" (1984, 52). The government was essentially prohibiting the refugees from planting any firm roots that might encourage permanence. Such roots, however, might have reinforced the already formed Maya identity or created new ones, either of which allow a renewed strength on the part of the refugees.

In his description of the China camp (a temporary camp used en route to Campeche), Clay comments that the refugees were housed in "two large concrete warehouses" (1984b, 53). Placing two thousand refugees in two warehouses eliminates any sense of privacy and tears away at the domesticity of the family. Overcrowdedness in circumstances such as these breaks down lines of solidarity and confuses one's sense of being and connection to which identity can be attached. In reaction to this overcrowdedness, the Maya used the same tactics as the Palestinians. "Families from the same villages in Guatemala or at least the same camps in Chiapas have remained close to each other in the warehouses, in effect constructing villages without walls" (Clay 1984b, 53).

Mexican authorities also deprived the refugees of food through restricted food rations (Clay 1984a, 1984b; Manz 1984). COMAR officials viewed this as a method for pushing refugees into relocating to Campeche or going back to Guatemala. Humanitarian organizations, on the other hand, charged COMAR with using food as a weapon to force refugees into being complacent and amenable to the goals of the host authorities (Clay 1984a).

It is fair to note that the Mexican government and COMAR did not always act this way. The construction of the forest camps in Campeche were sites where COMAR wanted the refugees to have a permanent habitation. These camps were literally "carved out of the forest" (Clay 1984b, 54). Mexicans provided streets and house frames, and the refugees were to build the rest of the house structures. Their movement was not restricted, and the refugees gained a sense of freedom and security. Maya families were able to live in private homes. Even then, with the freedoms that such a community allowed, "the houses of people from the same villages are side by side" (Clay 1984b, 54).

The forest community became a symbolic dichotomy between the host country, allowing the assimilation process to occur, and the refugees, who were still struggling to retain their identity from their original homelands. The Mexican authorities and COMAR see such cities as "permanent" refugee camps. The question remains: given the fact that the Maya attempted to recreate their home villages within these camps, will the refugees willingly remain in Mexico or will they, like other displaced Maya, struggle with repatriation or resettlement, either of which involves the transformation of identities?

Palestinians, on the other hand, did not actively seek resettlement into a third country. Instead of losing power within the refugee camp, Palestinians gained control of their identities through their resistance movement "in spite of twenty-four-hour surveillance of the camp by high-tech telescopes, the ringing of the camp with guard towers and regular army patrols through its streets" (Peteet 1995b, 175). Palestinian control over the camps created another borderland situation by exacerbating the us-them distinction between Palestinians and their Lebanese hosts.

In Lebanon, "urban Lebanese neighborhoods" were found at the "margins" of the Palestinian camps, where, according to Julie Peteet,

> Danger lurks here in the form of Lebanese militias and armed civilians who, since 1982, have beaten, kidnapped, detained, and killed Palestinians. Living in such a "perilous territory of not-belonging" is more than a state of mind, a sense of alienation and difference; it also signifies danger and exposure, a stripping away of the protection that can come from belonging to an internationally recognized state. (1995b, 175)

Communalism has also served as a survival technique in intentional communities, especially in the formative years. Before the means of subsistence is firmly established, communal sharing may be the most effective way of not only sharing identity but economic hardship as well. But such communalism can lead to the subordination of personal identity to group requirements. The institutionalization of communal power and loss of personal identity were symbolically enacted at Oneida as new members were required to deny their old way of life and to "deliver all worldly possessions to the group, to purge themselves completely of their conceptions of their personality and to swallow imposed regulations without challenge or even doubt" (Fellman 1973, 50; see also Foster 1984 and 1991). Upon joining the community, the individual's place was redefined, as was his or her identity.

For example, members of the Oneida community were required to participate in and uphold four community institutions: (1) the system of "complex marriage" (group marriage) in which all adult members of the community were married to each other; (2) "male continence," constituting a form of *coitus reservatus* as a form of birth control; (3) "stirpiculture," a form of eugenics, enforced by Noyes, which forced individuals to procreate without the choice of a partner—enacted for the good of the community; (4) communal raising of children. All members were required to adjust themselves to these four institutions, regardless of their personal feelings in the matter. Whether these constituted mild or severe restrictions upon the individual depended on the degree to which the member supported the goals of the community.

On the other hand, rules and regulations can as easily promote group identity by instituting fewer or more liberal rules than the larger society. At Hopedale, the regulations that guided members stipulated that they not "hate, injure, or kill anyone, even any enemy, and even in self-defense; furthermore, they could not vote, serve in military, or use any governmental agency, including courts" (Kesten 1993, 21–22).

The labor of individuals living at Brook Farm was all volunteer. These individuals were also free to choose the type of work they performed. The cooperative's labor system was divided into different "departments" (Spann 1989, 58). Each department was then controlled by a director who became responsible for the duties under the department. Although these duties were under the control of the director, he left the work to be completed by volunteers. Each individual at Brook Farm was *obligated* to provide sixty hours of labor per week in the summer and forty-eight hours per week in the winter (Spann 1989, 58–59).

Initially, this labor system was seen as being beneficial to the community as a whole and to the individual. Soon, however, individuals lost their enthusiasm for being a part of the community's labor system and the community itself. Spann notes that the "members seemed to lose some of their zeal as they settled into their new routines; enjoyable work did not necessarily mean productive labor, nor did communal picnics necessarily make for a deep commitment to brotherhood" (1989, 63).

Some communes have been institutionalized along authoritarian and patriarchal lines. In Brook Farm, for example, women were hard workers and were very capable of leadership, yet they were put under the control of dominating male leaders and were often "nearly powerless, submitting to a male-dominated regime in ideology, work, and sexual relations" (Chmielewski, Kern, and Klee-Hartzell 1993, 190; Kesten 1993, 101).

INCORPORATION: FINDING A NEW IDENTITY

> The ritual subject, individual or corporate, is in a stable state once more and by virtue of this has rights and obligations of a clearly defined and "structural" type, and is expected to behave in accordance with certain customary norms and ethical standards.
>
> —Victor Turner

Residence in refugee camps and intentional communities is often not permanent. While it is true that most refugee camps eventually close down, it is also true that most communes fall short of their utopian goals and dissolve. If they last, they generally settle into a permanent form that is different from the early, transitional phase. The liminal state is always temporary—a transition through which an old identity is transformed into a new identity. Borderlands are transient—a stage of transition in which life and identity are fluid and in which shifts in culture take place. They are home to traveling caravans of culture and society in which the borderlands serve as an intersection between crossroads headed toward different destinations. Refugee camps and intentional communities form an intermediary position through which the refugee relocates and the communard searches on. Because they are transitional, they often do not survive.

However, the liminal state can be an extended one. Some refugee camps hang on through long periods of time while battles are fought and won or lost, or as refugees make their way with their new identities to a new society in which still another transition is necessary before coming to terms with a stable new identity. In the case of the Palestinians, their new identity was a reinforcement of the old. Palestinians refused to resettle and to repatriate. Either option was viewed as legitimizing the state that expelled them. Throughout this span of rootless suffering, the Palestinians have been able to regenerate their nationalist struggle and pass it on to their offspring. After the war of 1967, the Palestinian resistance movement grew with youthful support, and the *intifada* (Palestinian uprising) of the 1980s revitalized their solidarity and their identity. Generations perceived themselves not as victims per se but as "Palestinian, struggler, revolutionary" (Sayigh 1979, 166).

When they resettle in a new country, refugees become strangers in a strange land and, in many cases, find themselves relegated to minority status, unable to communicate in a foreign language, and unfamiliar with local customs. Because of this, the refugee enters a new borderland in which his or her place and identity become redefined once again. Allan F. Burns described the relocation of the Maya to the community of Indiantown, Florida:

> They have gone through changes in their external identity from welcome strangers to tolerated farmworkers, to disliked "invaders." Internally, they have changed from refugees shocked by their experience to a diverse community of surviving Maya. (1993, 131)

The resettlement of the Hmong in the United States provides an example of how incorporation, or aggregation, affects identity through generational levels. Children who received their education in the United States became acculturated more quickly than their elders, creating contradictions and conflict between elders who clung to Hmong values and youngsters who chose U. S. values (Chan 1994, 55).

In addition, roles within the family changed as children, who spoke English, became intermediaries between older Hmong and Americans. The male struggle for patriarchal control within the presumed equality of American culture was a losing battle, because bride kidnapping, wife beating, and polygamy were now unacceptable practices in the dominant culture, permitting American authorities to intervene in what was previously Hmong private domestic space. The elderly suffered too. "The most painful moments they endure, however, occur when their own children and grandchildren no longer consult them, listen to their advice, or show them any respect" (Chan 1994, 57; see also Donnelly 1994).

Intentional communities that began as communal societies sometimes end or shift their emphasis to a more individualistic way of life in order to continue. Communities such as Oneida, Hopedale, and Brook Farm were constructed as retreats from a spoiled society and were seen as the means to reconstitute society as a whole through the mending of its ailments (Fogarty 1990, 215). Popular among these communities was the idea of individuals sacrificing themselves for the needs of the community, which also led to improved individuals. The benefits of the community were thought to leave their residue upon the individual.

However, through daily routines, life chances, and the competing shadow of the outside world, individuals often become pressured into ranking their needs over those of the community. This led to the separation of one's identity from that of the community, creating a dual consciousness. The giving of the body, whether it was for procreation at Oneida, labor at Brook Farm, or religion at Ballou's Hopedale, forced some individuals into conflict (Ballou 1972; Fellman 1973; Foster 1984, 1991; Spann 1989). The reaction to this conflict of commitment has often led to the eventual demise of most intentional communities (see Kanter 1973, 445).

The fate of the Oneida community is a complex issue containing various elements. The first pressure originated in the outside society. As with all communities, Oneida could not escape the economic and legal boundaries of its surrounding environment (see Janzen 1981). Financially caught inside the cage of capitalism, Oneida realized that in order to survive, discretionary resources had to be mobilized. By mere coincidence, the 1850s brought the converted Sewell Newhouse to the Oneida community. Sewell was a trapper and "brought with him designs for efficient steel animal traps" (Fellman 1973, 57–58). These traps were secured through patents and were marketed by Oneida to the entire nation. A factory was built for the demands of the nation and resulted in Noyes employing outside labor. The community members soon found themselves working for profit, which eventually led to the rise of private property and individual rather than group marriages.

A more important crisis arose within Oneida based on generational differences. Michael Fellman tells us: "The second generation of Noyes' followers, who were the first to be born at Oneida, lacked the zeal of the original converts, their parents" (1973, 58). Over fifty children were of this generation. With the aging of Noyes and his hierarchy, control shifted toward these individuals. Noyes's system of stirpiculture, complex marriage, and mutual criticism reached its upper limits in the community. "After years of smoldering resentment, the young men in the community finally opened a rebellion against Noyes and the other aging fathers of Oneida" (Fellman 1973, 60). By 1879, pressure from the second generation forced Noyes into fleeing to Canada, where he stayed until his death. Once Noyes had departed, individuals engaged in legal marriages and private property became an increasing demand. The idea of turning to private property and marriages only supports the claim that the Oneida community shifted its identity when communalism was no longer required for survival.

In contrast to Oneida, the fate of Brook Farm was out of the control of its inhabitants. Spann (1989) lists three reasons why Brook Farm dismantled. First, in 1845, an epidemic of varioloid (a variant of smallpox) hit Brook Farm with great force. The impact of this outbreak did not lead to any deaths, but it "paralyzed the community and disrupted its school" (1989, 95). With the Farm production virtually frozen, the costs of medical attention and the loss of income placed a large financial burden upon the Farm. This financial burden was also the second cause of the downfall of the community, according to Spann. He states that sustaining the community had an "expensive price which they [the members] had to strain every resource to meet" (1989, 95). The final stage of their demise came in 1846 with a disastrous fire that destroyed a large section of their compound. Without insurance, Brook Farm was forced to close its doors and have its members go their separate ways.

Ballou's reflection on Hopedale and its closure in 1856 directs the responsibility of closure to both the individuals of the community and the outside world. His first remark is that the members "lacked Christlike values and virtue necessary to the successful prosecution and final triumph of such an undertaking" (1972, 348–49). He felt he had been premature in believing that he and his followers would be able to recreate heaven on earth. Ballou also felt that it was the world's fault that such an endeavor could not survive: the world itself was not ready for divine individuals to reform a society filled with amoral atrocities.

Among his other causes for the closing of Hopedale was a restrictive constitution. "Our Constitution and general polity under it were too rigid and inflexible, making too little allowance for individual tastes, capabilities, adaptations, judgements, choice of action and occupation, etc." (1972, 363). The founder also viewed capitalism and its lure of his followers as being another destructive influence. Members made contacts with the outside world, thereby receiving descriptions of materialistic and profitable livelihoods. It is rational for Ballou to explain the closing of Hopedale for religious reasons. This gave legitimacy to his personal ideologies and the community identity while giving less importance to individual desires and needs.

The second generation of Oneida individuals were faced with an alien world, a world they took advantage of through private property and legal marriages. Identity for them transformed itself from that of a collective identity of community to that of individual citizens of the community at large, taking refuge in the nuclear family. Movement for these individuals was preferable to living under the oppressive rule of Noyes.

Destruction at Brook Farm, on the other hand, forced individuals to move into the outside world. Living in the outside world after leaving the communal life presents different dimensions of the identity struggle that comes with incorporation. The memoirs of John Thomas Codman present reflections on the hardships and the simplicities of incorporating themselves into their new environment. Some of the members anxiously traveled to California to take part in the Gold Rush (Codman 1894, 243).

Actions like this are similar to what happened at the Oneida community. The question arises as to why individuals, who were living in a communal state where individuals lived for the community, felt the need to take part in a scheme to find personal wealth? Was Brook Farm more repressive to the individual than previously thought? It is hard to say with only letters and memoirs as sources of data. Codman himself describes his sadness in leaving and how it was only his physical presence that was absent from Brook Farm (1894, 232).

The possibilities of life after communal existence are limiting. In fact, I can think of only four, one of which is death. First, there is the attempt to incorporate oneself into the larger society. Codman recalls that the shoemakers of Brook Farm were able to find jobs successfully (1894, 233). Second, individuals who were unsuccessful at, or feared, incorporation searched for other intentional communities. This was also the case for some of the members of Brook

Farm who joined with the North American Phalanx (1894, 243). Identity then becomes transposed into a different space, but people retain the same sentiments held previously. Third, individuals become isolated from society and from communities. Implicit in this is the need for sustenance, which inevitably requires either dependence upon the outside world or at least minimal contact, either of which can influence a change in the identity of the individual and estrangement from both types of communities.

Human suffering leads people into the existence of refugees and to alternative ways of living in communal societies, but these two states of existence have in common the quest for identity, its loss, its resurrection, and its reconstruction. The purpose of this comparison has not been to disparage the controversial politics or human suffering experienced by refugees, nor to trivialize the often fleeting attempts at communal existence that dot the landscape of human history. Instead, I have shown how the cultural categories of borderlands and communalism are comparable in their implications for human beings striving to meet the challenges of conflict and change. Through the understanding of the experience of liminality, we can understand the common struggles that human beings experience in their attempts to hold on to their identities in the midst of change.

Acknowledgments

I would like to thank the following individuals: Julie Peteet for her insightful comments and lectures on refugee studies, and Susan Love Brown for the opportunity, patience, and support in writing this essay. Earlier versions of this paper were presented at the 1995 Communal Studies Association meeting and the 1996 North Central Sociology Association conference.

Reference List

Anzaldua, Gloria. 1987. *Borderlands: La Frontera*. San Francisco: Aunt Lute Books.

Ballou, Adin. 1972. *History of the Hopedale Community, From its Inception to its Virtual Submergence in the Hopedale Parish*. Philadelphia: Porcupine Press.

Burns, Allan F. 1993. *Maya in Exile: Guatemalans In Florida*. Philadelphia: Temple University Press.

Chan, Suchang, ed. 1994. *Hmong Means Free: Life in Laos and America*. Philadelphia: Temple University Press.

Chmielewski, Wendy E., Louis J. Kern, and Marlyn Klee-Hartzell, eds. 1993. *Women in Spiritual and Communitarian Societies in the United States*. Syracuse, N.Y.: Syracuse University Press.

Clay, Jason W. 1984a. Guatemalan Refugees in Mexico. *Cultural Survival Quarterly* 8, no. 3:46–49.

———. 1984b. The Campeche Camps. *Cultural Survival Quarterly* 8, no. 3:53–54.

Codman, John Thomas. 1894. *Brook Farm: Historic and Personal Memoirs*. Boston: Arena.

Donnelly, Nancy D. 1994. *Changing Lives of Refugee Hmong Women*. Seattle: University of Washington Press.

Earle, Duncan M. 1988. Mayas Aiding Mayas: Guatemalan Refugees in Chiapas, Mexico. In *Harvest of Violence: The Maya Indians and the Guatemalan Crisis,* edited by Robert M. Carmack. Norman: University of Oklahoma Press.

Fellman, Michael. 1973. *The Unbounded Frame: Freedom and Community in Nineteenth Century American Utopianism*. Westport, Conn.: Greenwood Press.

Ferris, Elizabeth G. 1987. *The Central American Refugees*. New York: Praeger.

Fogarty, Robert S. 1990. *All Things New: American Communes and Utopian Movements, 1860–1914*. Chicago: University of Chicago Press.

Foster, Lawrence. 1984. *Religion and Sexuality: The Shakers, the Mormons, and the Oneida Community*. Urbana: University of Illinois Press.

———. 1991. *Women, Family, and Utopia: Communal Experiments of the Shakers, the Oneida Community, and the Mormons*. Syracuse, N.Y.: Syracuse University Press.

Hendricks, Glenn L., and Bruce T. Downing. 1986. *The Hmong in Transition*. New York: The Center for Migration Studies.

Hostetler, John A. 1974. *Communitarian Societies*. New York: Holt, Rinehart, and Winston.

Janzen, Donald. 1981. The Intentional Community-National Interface: An Approach to the Study of Communal Societies. *Communal Societies* 1:37–42.

Kanter, Rosabeth Moss, ed. 1973. *Communes: Creating and Managing the Collective Life*. New York: Harper & Row.

Kesten, Seymour R. 1993. *Utopian Episodes: Daily Life in Experimental Colonies Dedicated to Changing the World*. Syracuse, N.Y.: Syracuse University Press.

Long, Lynellyn D. 1993. *Ban Vinai: The Refugee Camp*. New York: Columbia University Press.

Malkki, Lisa. 1992. National Geographic: Rooting of Peoples and the Territorialization of National Identity among Scholars and Refugees. *Cultural Anthropology* 7, no. 1:24–44.

Manz, Beatriz. 1984. The Forest Camps in Eastern Chiapas, Mexico. *Cultural Survival Quarterly* 8, no. 3:50–52.

———. 1988. *Refugees of a Hidden War: The Aftermath of Counterinsurgency in Guatemala*. Albany: State University of New York Press.

Peteet, Julie. 1995a. Personal communications with the author.

———. 1995b. Transforming Trust: Dispossession and Empowerment among Palestinian Refugees. In *Mistrusting Refugees*., edited by E. Valentine Daniel and John Chr. Knudsen. Berkeley: University of California Press.

Sayigh, Rosemary. 1979. *Palestinians: From Peasants to Revolutionaries*. London: Zed Books.

Schiff, Benjamin N. 1995. *Refugees unto the Third Generation: UN Aid to Palestinians*. Syracuse, N.Y.: Syracuse University Press.

Spann, Edward K. 1989. *Brotherly Tomorrows: Movements for a Cooperative Society in America, 1820–1920*. New York: Columbia University Press.

Tuan, Yi-fu. 1977. *Space and Place: The Perspective of Experience*. Minneapolis: University of Minnesota Press.

Turner, Victor. 1964. Betwixt and Between: The Liminal Period in "Rites de Passage." In *Symposium on New Approaches to the Study of Religion: Proceedings of the 1964 Annual Spring Meeting of the American Ethnological Society*. Seattle: University of Washington Press.

U. S. Committee for Refugees. 1995. World Refugee Survey Immigration and Refugee Services of America.

Van Gennep, Arnold. 1960. *The Rites of Passage*. Chicago: University of Chicago Press.

Walker-Moffat, Wendy. 1995. *The Other Side of the Asian American Success Story*. San Francisco: Jossey-Bass.

Zolberg, Aristide R., Astri Suhrke, and Sergio Aguayo. 1989. *Escape from Violence: Conflict and the Refugee Crisis in the Developing World*. New York: Oxford University Press.

⁜6⁜

The Mob at Enfield: Community, Gender, and Violence against the Shakers

Elizabeth A. De Wolfe

This week we have been very much disturbed by day and nights," wrote a worried Shaker sister in 1818. "This [disturbance] to us appeared an alarming circumstance as we were left almost without protection" (Statement 1818). The anonymous author of this manuscript recollection, "A Statement concerning the Mob at Enfield," had reason for fear. Since the Shakers first practiced their sectarian faith in postrevolutionary New England, they had been the target of public scorn and collective violence. From harassing mobs that stoned and assaulted founder Ann Lee and her followers on their proselytizing journey of 1780–84, to an enormous group of more than five hundred individuals that assailed the Shaker settlement in Union Village, Ohio, the nonbelieving public used the power of collective activity to force Shakers to act more compatibly with societal norms. In 1818, public opinion turned against the Shakers at Enfield, New Hampshire, and for five days, a mob set fear into the heart of the Shakers. The Mob at Enfield can be read as a social drama, a multiphase social action wherein opposing groups attempt to negotiate a resolution to troubling social conflict.

Emerging in the American colonies in 1774, Shakerism quickly spread with the winds of religious revivals across New England, into Ohio, Kentucky, and Indiana, and eventually, briefly, south to Georgia and Florida (Brewer 1986; Stein 1992). At its mid-nineteenth-century peak, Shakerism encompassed some four thousand members in nineteen communities. Shakers lived in communal villages apart from the surrounding populace. All property was shared and biological kin relations were abandoned in favor of the community-wide family of brothers and sisters.

Shakerism is a Protestant faith whose members believe that the Second Coming of Christ occurred within individuals open to His spirit (Johnson 1969). To work toward the indwelling of the Christ spirit, Shakers attempt to live a Christlike life, practicing confession of sins and celibacy. Shakers also espoused gender equality, a reflection of their belief that the Godhead has both masculine and feminine characteristics. Although work roles within Shaker communities were divided along traditional gender lines, leadership positions were held in pairs with a male and female leader. Such beliefs and practices—celibacy, confession, communalism, a female leader, and the Shakers' view of the Second Coming—ran contrary to the cultural norms of patriarchy and Protestantism. This conflict was the basis of mob attacks and other acts designed to suppress Shakerism.

The Mob at Enfield, a multiday event, was a powerful social drama which called to the forefront community standards concerning the rights of mothers and the limits of religious tolerance. As Victor Turner has defined it, the social drama is an exceptional moment in human activity, an "aharmonic or disharmonic process" (Turner 1974, 37) and "often [the social drama] is a question of one cultural rule opposing another" (Turner 1984, 20). The drama is initiated by a breach of a social norm or a "crucial bond" among the members of the community at large (Turner 1984, 19). The breach widens to a crisis in which members of the wide community are split into opposing camps. During this fractious stage, individuals group and regroup as the breach expands to encompass additional grievances or agenda. This "highly contagious" period segments the community and reduces shades of opinion to more stark opposites of black and white (Turner 1984, 23). In the Mob at Enfield, the gender and marital status of the mob's instigators affected the changing level of public support for their cause. Further, the different physical locations for each act in the multiday mob added additional symbolic meaning to the event; space and place are thus potent players in this social drama.

The crisis is addressed when participants in a highly reflexive state look back upon their selves and situation and attempt to rectify the breach and restore order. Through appeals to tradition, legal action, or decisions from leaders, the resolution lays bare the heart of the tension and attempts to heal the wound. The social drama reaches its finale with some sort of outcome from the attempted resolution. The outcome, though, is unpredictable—the group may split apart or may coalesce—and thus the social drama is a powerful, tension-filled, unpredictable arena of human activity.

The anonymous Shaker quoted above captured the fluid nature of the social drama in the manuscript account penned to record the event. The document, one of two from Shaker hands likely written as part of formal proceedings to protest the mob action, offers a valuable insider's view from the Shaker perspective (Statement 1818; Lyon 1818). The mob's perspective is equally enlightening, and the mob event is recorded in the work of anti-Shaker authors Mary Marshall Dyer (herself an instigator of the mob) and Abram Van Vleet, an Ohio publisher (Dyer 1822, 1847; Van Vleet 1818).

In addition, a subsequent petition to the 1818 New Hampshire legislature reveals the nature of the incident from the perspective of forty-eight residents of the town of Enfield (in Dyer 1818, 34–35). In this analysis, each document serves as an insider's account from various positions, both geographical and conceptual. Teasing out the information held within each work, keeping in mind the bias each author retains, provides evocative data for a historical ethnography of this dramatic event.

In the social drama that the Shakers would subsequently call the "Mob at Enfield," the subject's position determines the nature of the conflict. In applying Turner's stages of social drama to this event, we must look at each stage from multiple venues. From the perspective of the village of Enfield, the breach centered on Shaker treatment of nonbelieving wives of Shaker husbands and these mothers' access to their Shaker-held children. Abandoned by their husbands and left without property or protection, wives turned to the non-Shaker community to help them gain redress. The Shakers, however, saw the conflict through the eyes of their communal society. From their perspective, the breach centered on religious tolerance and their right to organize their society as they desired.

Similarly, the mounting crisis divided the community into several factions. The crisis poised the Shakers and their supporters (sympathetic townspeople) against certain members of the town of Enfield, some local officials, and two women—Mary Marshall Dyer and Eunice Hawley Chapman, whose husbands and children lived with the Enfield Shakers. These alliances were by no means static, and allegiances rapidly shifted as the drama unfolded over several days. These shifts were highly instructive in understanding the internal dynamics of this multilayered event. These shifts also reveal specific subagendas that were caught up during the contagious crisis phrase. For example, several townspeople were less concerned with the fate of the Dyer or Chapman children than they were about the potential economic burden they would face supporting the distressed mothers who could become the new town poor.

In attempting to resolve the conflict, a local judge's verdict supported the concerns of all involved—religious rights, mother's rights, economic concerns—yet this outcome in effect only placed a small plug in a large hole. His decision brought this particular drama to a close and restored stability to the wider community of Enfield. But the particulars of his decision also guaranteed further instability by suggesting alternative arenas for dispute, acknowledging and legitimizing the conflict between communal group and surrounding community.

Collective activity in the form of a social drama, such as the Mob at Enfield, is an act of social criticism against communalism. Understanding the dynamics of this critique elucidates the relationship between communal groups and the surrounding dominant culture. Examining such conflict as a performance can inform us of the boundaries of social practice and the limits of tolerance between not only Shakers and the surrounding people they called the "World," but between any communal group and the dominant community they in part or in whole reject.

The social drama is a public performance. On the one hand, it follows a cultural script which makes comparison with other anticommunal acts possible. On the other hand, the script is not cast in stone, and thus activity can, and does, vary. This in fact is the power of the social drama and one the Shaker observer recognized: the outcome of the scenario was unknown and therefore appeared "an alarming circumstance" (Statement 1818).

Mobs as public performance

The chaotic appearance of a mob masks an underlying order, pattern, and rationale (Gilje 1987; Richards 1970; Rudé 1981; Weinbaum 1979; Woods 1983). Mobs against the Shakers were multiday events with alternating periods of intensive activity and quiet inactivity. Often the participants returned to their homes between periods of attack. Each mob event featured a core group of leaders who organized the mob, led the group to the site, made demands, and controlled (albeit tenuously) the action. In addition to the leaders, an assortment of participants formed a potentially dangerous and highly excitable supporting cast.

As Rudé (1981) and Woods (1983) have illustrated, the crowd comprises individuals with diverse backgrounds, occupations, and interests. This crowd is more than a faceless mass moving as if by an unseen force; the crowd is an integral component of a complex event set in a specific historical context. The larger the crowd, the more potential for a dangerous, uncontrolled explosion of fury as subgroups of the larger assembly pushed their own issues during the conflict.

Frequently, Shaker apostates or biological relatives of Shakers raised the anti-Shaker mob. While the apostates rarely received their demands for back pay or goods, mobs that attempted to retrieve Shaker-held children were frequently successful, usually because the large number of participants overwhelmed the Shaker group and simply grabbed the child (or children) and ran. In all mobs, the potential for violence was quite real. Mobs injured Shakers, harmed animals, and destroyed property. Shakers were kept well informed of the anti-Shaker activities inflicted upon their sister communities through frequent correspondence. Thus, when the Enfield Shakers learned of the gathering mob, they were well aware of the actions to come through experience with numerous previous dramas.

The Enfield mob event was multilayered, somewhat complicating Turner's process. In the broadest view, the Shakers and the surrounding townspeople formed one large community that shared the same geographic address of Enfield, New Hampshire. This small town lay in southwestern New Hampshire eight miles east of the Connecticut River. The Enfield Shakers first entered into a communal living style there in 1793 and while at first, as at most other Shaker sites, there was considerable hostility toward the sect, by the 1810s the Shakers and their neighbors lived in more or less peaceful coexistence. The Enfield Shaker "village" of roughly 150 members, situated on the shore of Mascoma Lake, formed a segregated group within the larger community of the town of Enfield.

In addition to geographic locale, the Shakers and surrounding townspeople shared a history, business relationships, and a few kin connections by way of the local townspeople who had converted to Shakerism. The mob event split the larger community into two main camps: those supporting the Shakers, and those opposed.

According to Turner the breach initiates the social drama (Turner 1974, 38). But here, in fact, it is a mere point of departure. The breach between the Shakers and the village of Enfield had been long-standing. The Shakers, by their communal style of living and their disavowal of the marriage bond, had disregarded the social norm of the patriarchal, conjugal family. The stability achieved between the Shakers and the town was actually an agreement to accept the breach as a norm. The relationship between communal group and host community was permanently in a heightened state. What moved the social drama from breach to crisis was the agitating presence of the coleaders of the mob, Eunice Hawley Chapman and Mary Marshall Dyer, whose husbands and eight children lived among the Enfield Shakers.

Chapman and Dyer initiated the 1818 mob with their public pleas for assistance. In the period of crisis, townspeople and some local officials united around the complaint of the poor treatment Shakers gave to women whose husbands and children remained with the sect. The mob sought to force the Shakers to provide financial support for nonbelieving wives and, specifically, to release the children of Mary Dyer and Eunice Chapman. On the surface, the mob questioned the obligations a community (communal or otherwise) had to its members. On a deeper level, the mob event revealed not only the town's concern for the Shakers' moral and ethical behavior but also a fundamental concern with the financial impact Shaker defections would have on their town.

The mob event thus began with a widening of the breach. The situation of a communal sect within a larger community (the village of Enfield) moved from tenuous stability to growing instability when Chapman and Dyer revived long-standing complaints about Shaker belief and practices, including the separation of mothers from children. The mounting crisis grew as additional individuals took up the cause and added concerns of their own, such as the fear of an increased tax burden in order to provide for the women, such as Dyer, abandoned by their Shaker husbands. The Shakers responded to the crisis with their issues: that Dyer and Chapman were not members of their group and thus were beyond their concern, and, more fundamentally, that the townspeople had breached the town-communal group stability by threatening to meddle in internal Shaker affairs.

Shaker Husbands, Worldly Wives

Like many women caught in the religious revivals that swept northern New England in the first decade of the nineteenth century, Mary Marshall Dyer (1780–1867) sought salvation. She thought she had found it when an itinerant preacher introduced Shakerism to her northern New Hampshire community. Mary and her husband, Joseph, read a Shaker book, visited a Shaker community, and hosted a visit from two Shaker leaders. In the winter of 1813, Joseph, Mary, their five children (ranging in age from four to thirteen years), and nearly two dozen of their neighbors traveled more than one hundred miles to the south and joined the Enfield, New Hampshire, Shakers.

At first, both Mary and Joseph found satisfaction with their new Shaker lives. Joseph appreciated the rigid, hierarchical community whose order and discipline had been lacking in his troubled marriage. Mary, already in a highly awakened religious state, appreciated the opportunity to speak openly on religious matters and imagined herself quickly becoming one of the Shakers' female ministers. In 1814 Joseph and Mary formally indentured their children to the Shakers, a standard practice in which the Shakers agreed to care for the children's basic needs, provide a practical education, and train them in a trade. The children would remain with the Shakers until they reached the age of majority, at which time the children were free to leave or to join the communal, celibate sect.

However, shortly after executing this contract, Mary began to drift away from Shakerism, growing increasingly dissatisfied with her slow progress toward a leadership role. By the winter of 1815, Mary had decided to leave, and since she had been a most troublesome novice, neither the Shaker leaders nor her estranged husband, Joseph, attempted to dissuade her. But when Mary requested the return of her children, Joseph and the Elders refused, setting Mary on a highly visible, highly vocal public campaign of anti-Shakerism (De Wolfe 1996).

While Mary Dyer fought the Shakers for the return of her children in New Hampshire, James and Eunice Chapman waged a similar battle in the New York state legislature. Unable to endure his failed marriage, James abandoned his family. After working several jobs along the Hudson River, James became acquainted with the Shakers at Watervliet, New York. Believing his wife was unable to care properly for his children, James traveled to his former home and, while Eunice was away, whisked the three children off to the Watervliet Shakers.

When Eunice begged for their return, James refused, prompting Eunice to begin a public, aggressive campaign that included publishing two anti-Shaker pamphlets, writing threatening letters to Shaker leaders, and petitioning the New York legislature for a divorce from James and the return of her children (Chapman 1817, 1818). Newspapers in New York and New England followed her campaign. When the legislature granted Eunice's requests, the children were nowhere to be found and the Shakers claimed no knowledge of their whereabouts. Unbeknownst to most everyone in New York, James Chapman and the children were in hiding at the Enfield, New Hampshire, Shaker community (Blake 1960; Humez 1994).

The Mob at Enfield, New Hampshire

The Enfield mob did not erupt spontaneously in May of 1818. Acting on a tip that her children were hidden in New Hampshire, Eunice Chapman traveled to Enfield and arrived in mid-May. Although she journeyed undercover, local residents discovered her identity and purpose and sent for Mary Dyer, who had established her identity as an anti-Shaker leader with a petition to the New Hampshire legislature the previous year. This was the first meeting of Chapman and Dyer, although the two women had corresponded with one another for several months. Eunice and Mary stayed at a local inn belonging to an opponent of Shakerism, James Willis. There they made a plan to retrieve their children, confiding only in those whom they believed could help them and enlarging their group as the perceived breach of the Shakers' neglect of the mother-child bond widened into crisis. Restoring the mothers' children would resolve this crisis and end the social drama.

The initial scheme called for Dyer and several women to travel to the Shakers and request a visit with the Dyer children. Once admitted, the group would request to see Chapman's children as well. At that point Eunice would take the Shakers by surprise, bursting in on the assembly and snatching away her children. One of the Dyer-Chapman confidants, however, alerted the Shakers to the impending visit and that knowledge forced Mary and Eunice to alter their strategy to a more direct approach.

On Monday, 25 May, the Shakers learned that Eunice and Mary "with their forces" of supportive townspeople planned to come to the village the following morning at 8:00 A.M. (Statement 1818). The Shakers had good reason to worry about the gathering mob, since several of the male leaders and Joseph Dyer were absent from the Shaker village. In an attempt to preempt violence, the Shakers asked Enfield resident Judge Evans to speak to Eunice and Mary and reach a compromise on visiting the children. Chapman refused to bargain, as she intended not to go to the Shakers unless she could take away her children. Evans, who had previously assisted Mary Dyer in her attempts to visit her children, agreed to escort Chapman to the Shakers the following morning.

At this crisis stage of the drama, the Shakers appealed to Evans for resolution, and Evans, as a legal authority, acted in that role. As Turner notes (1984, 24), in the resolution phase "the aim . . . is to diffuse tension" and "reconcile conflicting parties." As a mediator, Evans worked for both the Shakers and the townspeople under the assumption "that it is better to restore a state of peace than to continue in a state of hostility" (Turner 1984, 24). To prevent Eunice Chapman (and perhaps Mary Dyer) from grabbing the children, Evans would accompany her to protect the Shakers. Simultaneously, to prevent the Shakers from refusing the mothers a visit with their children, Evans would accompany the women. Although Chapman had initially refused to bargain, by late Monday, 25 May, she had agreed to Evans's proposal and the crisis shifted toward an apparent resolution.

On Tuesday morning, 26 May, Judge Evans returned to Willis's inn to escort Chapman but arrived to find a growing crowd. In the crowd was Joseph Merrill, an Enfield selectman and justice of the peace. Like Evans, Merrill had visited the Shakers the day before, and the Shakers had pleaded with him as "an officer of the peace" to quell the attack (Lyon 1818). But unlike Evans, and contrary to the Shakers' wishes, Merrill supported the notion of a show of town strength. The two attorneys argued with each other. Evans asserted that the Shakers would not permit such a large crowd of people to visit the children.

Acting as a self-appointed mediator, Evans drew up a list of proposed visitors that he carried out to the Shakers. But as Evans returned to the inn with the Shakers' counterproposal detailing who would be permitted to visit, he met Dyer and Chapman on the road. Unwilling to wait for a Shaker invitation, they were already headed toward the Shaker village with an entourage behind them, "some on gigs and some on horseback" (Statement 1818). Monday's resolution of a peaceable visit had deteriorated back to crisis as additional townspeople joined the women in their quest. Realizing his attempts at mediation had failed, Evans returned to town.

At the Shaker village both the mob and the Shakers vied to control the volatile situation. As Evans had earlier surmised, the Shakers refused to expose the Chapman and Dyer children to such a large number of excited visitors, fearful that, as had happened at other Shaker villages, the mob would simply surround the children and take them away. The Shakers agreed to permit a small contingent—Chapman and Dyer along with Selectman Merrill, Jesse Fogg (Enfield's representative to the legislature), and their wives—to visit the children in the Dwelling House. Chapman refused this offer and insisted the children be brought to her in the Trustee's Office.

The different physical locations in which each mob "act" occurred provided strategic advantages or disadvantages for the participants. The Dwelling House offered the Shakers both a symbolic and practical advantage. Symbolically, the Dwelling House represented the Shaker inner sanctum. In this private domain members of the Shaker family ate, slept, worked, and worshipped. Traditionally, only those individuals who were committed members were permitted within. Locating the visit in the Dwelling House increased the distinction between the outsider mothers and the insider children. It also separated the protagonists (Dyer and Chapman) from their potentially volatile supporters.

Practically, the Dwelling House was a relatively safer locale for the visit than the Trustee's Office, a betwixt and between location occupying the borderland between the Shaker community and the surrounding town community. In the Trustee's Office, the two communities came together during business transactions, trade, or visits. Acceding to Chapman's demands for a visit in the Trustee's Office would have lessened the "insider" status of the children. It would also place them physically closer to the boundary of the Shaker village, facilitating kidnapping and a quick escape.

The judges and their wives accepted the Shakers' offer and visited the children at the Dwelling House. After a short wait, Mary Dyer went to the Dwelling House. Finally, after a two-hour refusal and a personal invitation from her thirteen-year-old son George, Eunice Chapman made her way to the Dwelling House. The Shakers gained the first victory by forcing the visitors to go to the Dwelling House.

The visit exacted an emotional toll from both mothers. Eunice had not seen her children in over two years. When she saw her daughters, she wept uncontrollably—joyful at the reunion but fearful of the changes in their behavior. Her youngest daughter, Julia, refused to sit in her lap, and Susan, age twelve, became alarmed when Eunice removed Susan's Shaker cap. Although Eunice had brought a gift of a "handsome" doll, Julia ignored it. Both girls stated that they wished to remain with the Shakers.

Dyer's children's behavior distressed their mother as well. Betsy and Caleb Dyer, by then young adults, intervened between Mary and their younger siblings. Speaking for the five Dyer children they insisted that they were well cared for and satisfied with their Shaker lives. Mary's later recollection of this day focused on young Joseph (age eight) whom she held in her lap. In a clever use of Shaker phraseology, Mary asked Joseph if he would like to come and live with her "if it was the gift." The "gift" indicated a God-directed, Shaker Elder-sanctioned action, and thus young Joseph, fully socialized into Shaker life, responded "Yes" (Dyer 1822, 376).

At this point, Caleb, Betsy, and Shaker Nathaniel Draper whisked the youngster out of the room, angry at Mary's cleverness. Despite Mary's attempt to prove that her child wished to leave, the Shakers strained to keep an aura of civility in the proceedings and served supper to the six visitors before they returned to Enfield. Although Eunice, the Shakers recorded, spoke rudely, the judges and their wives appreciated the Shakers' hospitality. This concluded the visit.

The Shakers had forced a tenuous resolution to the crisis. The Shakers had conceded to the town's norm of maintaining biological kin ties and, in the presence of important witnesses, the Shakers had permitted the mothers to visit their children. Still, the supporting forces who had accompanied the women were denied entrance and the Shakers maintained the upper hand in controlling the activities within their own communal village. But one strained visit did not satisfy Dyer and Chapman; thus, the resolution was brief. This social drama continued to hover near crisis.

The drama continued late the following day, Wednesday, 27 May, and indicated the rapidly shifting power relationships. Having assembled "six or eight" women, Mary Dyer traveled to the Shaker village late in the day (Statement 1818). Compared to Chapman, Dyer had the weaker claim to see her children. She had signed the indenture papers and as yet did not have legal custody nor a legislative divorce. Local authorities hesitated to interfere in what was seen as a private marital dispute between Joseph and Mary. Her appearance at the Shakers without the accompaniment of authorities, or even any men, underscored her weaker position.

On the previous day, the Shakers had permitted Dyer a visit in a controlled situation with important witnesses present (thus showing their willingness to adhere to community norms). This time, the Shakers refused to let Mary enter the community. Angry at the insult, Mary Dyer threatened the Shakers, and with the principal male leaders away from the community, the warning rattled the Shakers. Well aware of Dyer's charismatic ability to stir up a crowd and fearing a night attack on the village, James Chapman hid his children.

The next afternoon, Eunice Chapman journeyed to the Shakers with local resident Samuel Cochran and his wife. She demanded to see her former husband, but James could not be found. The Shakers invited Eunice to wait for his return, but Eunice refused and instead stood in the road "hailing everyone that passed along, and telling them how bad the Shakers used her" (Statement 1818). Cochran and his wife left, but Eunice continued her public outcry until six in the evening.

News of the ruckus traveled back to town, and by evening Squire Merrill, Samuel Cochran, and twelve to fourteen men arrived at the Shaker village and demanded to see James Chapman. Merrill and Cochran led the group. Merrill made a long speech with many threats directed toward the Shakers. He began with an assertion that the group did not come for a riot, nor for the Dyer children. Merrill's statement signaled that Dyer would not have the support of the crowd that evening.

The crowd, Merrill asserted, sought the Chapman children and insisted upon a meeting with James, whom they implicitly recognized as possessing the power to release the children. Merrill stated loudly that James Chapman had escaped the laws of New York by fleeing to New Hampshire. James's escape from justice and the Shakers' refusal to help Eunice had "stirred up" people's minds. Merrill declared that the treatment of Eunice was "contrary to the laws of God and man" and the group would not leave until "satisfaction was given" (Statement 1818).

As darkness fell, more townspeople gathered at the Shaker community. One Shaker estimated that more than one hundred people surrounded the village. Some patrolled on horses and others hid under fences. Shaker John Lyon asked Merrill as an officer of the peace to disperse the crowd, but Merrill refused. Merrill spoke on behalf of the townspeople and took control of the escalating crisis. His long evening speech focused the demands of the mob on securing the Chapman children. Merrill simultaneously spoke for the crowd and to the crowd. In asserting that James Chapman was a fugitive from justice and should be removed from New Hampshire, Merrill focused the crowd's wrath on one individual, instead of on the Shakers in general.

In arguing that Eunice had been badly treated, Merrill kept the restoration of her children in the forefront, rather than provoking an assault on Shakerism. Merrill's long speech united the large crowd and prevented random mob violence by focusing attention on specific goals and by providing a time period during which hot tempers could cool. Consistent with nineteenth-century patterns of mob action where local authorities attempted to mediate between the mob's demands and those of their opponents, Merrill worked to enforce religious tolerance while still attending to local concerns. His refusal to disperse the crowd showed solidarity with his constituency and community values and ultimately prevented the collective group from degenerating into one hundred angry individuals. At the same time, Merrill's efforts maintained a level of religious and communal tolerance by acknowledging Shakerism in general. In his authoritative role, Merrill nudged the crisis toward resolution.

After dark, James Chapman appeared and met with Eunice in the North House shop. The volatile meeting continued until 11:00 P.M. This location is interesting. As a new member of the Shaker community, James lived with the North Family, a subset of the communal village in which novitiates were trained in Shaker thought, belief, and practice. Only when Shaker leaders had confidence in the seriousness and potential of a novitiate would that member move to another Shaker "family."

The fight in the North House shop underscores the Shakers' desire to distance themselves from the carnal world of marital discord. From the Shakers' perspective, the issue was retaining the children, to whom they believed they had some claim based on law (the Dyers' indenture) and custom (James's rights as father superseded Eunice's as a mother). The marital failures, what one Shaker would refer to as "domestic broils," of James and Eunice Chapman and Joseph and Mary Dyer were of little concern (McNemar 1819).

During the protracted debate, James and Eunice Chapman argued about the truth of her publications and a division of the children. Eunice suggested James could keep George, to whom she acknowledged he, as a father, had some claim, but she pleaded for the girls, invoking an early-nineteenth-century belief in the tender nature of young children and the delicate malleability of girls. While a crowd of townspeople looked on, the Chapmans argued, but failed to reach an agreement regarding the division of the children. Frustrated at the lack of compromise, Eunice Chapman and Squire Merrill (the latter perhaps in a bluff to force a resolution) threatened to bring five hundred people to the village the following day.

At 11:00 P.M. town officials produced a warrant for the arrest of James Chapman (for a charge unrelated to the mob), and he was taken away.[1] Some of the gathered crowd returned to their homes, interpreting the arrest as a legal resolution to the problem of James Chapman's behavior and to the crisis between the Shakers and the town. This subgroup of the mob recognized James Chapman as having the sole power to release the children; without James's authoritative presence, there was no other recourse but to leave the children with the Shakers. But others saw James's arrest as the removal of the last obstacle to obtaining the children. For this group, the crisis had moved to a different resolution: one of continued crisis for the Shakers. When Eunice announced she would not leave the Shaker village, the remaining crowd took matters into their own hands and searched the village for the children. Around 1:00 A.M. Enfield resident Moses Johnson discovered George Chapman hidden in a barn. Although she had hoped to retrieve her daughters as well, Eunice jumped into a waiting carriage and fled New Hampshire with George. With Eunice Chapman gone, the remainder of the mob broke up.

Three reasons motivated Eunice Chapman's rapid departure. First, George represented tangible proof that James had indeed removed the children from New York State. Upon her return to Albany, Eunice could thus receive a writ of habeas corpus to acquire, without a mob, her daughters. Second, Eunice likely realized that the aggressive means by which she ultimately recovered George was illegal, and it was best to absent herself from the fallout of such an action. Finally, and most importantly, George did not wish to leave the Shakers. When Eunice placed him in a carriage, he tried to escape. To prevent his return to the Shakers, either by his own volition or by the Shakers' attempt to retrieve him, Eunice placed as much distance as possible between George and Enfield.

The crisis phase of the social drama moved toward resolution on the following morning, Friday, 29 May. Since local officials had been unwilling or unable to resolve the situation informally, the Shakers lodged a formal complaint with Judge Blaisdell of the nearby village of Canaan. Blaisdell called together the principal participants, including Joseph Merrill, the Shaker leaders, and Mary Dyer. He rebuked the group for such a disorderly proceeding and especially castigated Merrill for failing to stop the unlawful search of the Shaker village.

Although she was not present at the meeting, Eunice Chapman received chastisement as well. When Blaisdell described Eunice Chapman as a "very bad character," Dyer spoke in her defense and argued that women like herself and Chapman were helpless against Shaker husbands (Dyer 1822, 378). After hearing Dyer's story, Blaisdell urged her to petition the legislature for assistance. Although Mary portrayed this incident in her later writings as evidence of Blaisdell's support against the Shakers, in reality Blaisdell urged the resolution of disputes through legal measures, rather than mob action. He did not disagree that Eunice had legal right to her children, but he opposed the method she used to assert that right.

Blaisdell's condemnation of Eunice Chapman and advice to Mary Dyer to seek redress through the legislature indicates the role that gender played in prompting the social drama at Enfield. Blaisdell implicitly argued that disputes, including those concerning mothers and children, would be best resolved by men acting with reason, rather than women acting from emotion. Gender and power intersected throughout this event. Dyer and Chapman drew upon the appearance of social powerlessness to gain access to power via Merrill, Evans, and local male residents. Dyer and Chapman invoked the potent cultural symbols of motherhood and their own femininity to reinforce their position. They understood themselves as being without authority to retrieve their own children and comprehended that to achieve their goals they must garner masculine assistance.

By emphasizing their position as mothers-without-children, Dyer and Chapman painted a picture of a disturbed domesticity where "private" women were forced into a "public" role in order to enact their "private" role as mothers. Their extraordinary foray into the public, masculine world of legislative petitions, book publication, and public speaking was motivated solely by a traditional feminine goal: to be mothers to their children. This breach of gender roles and resulting female visibility motivated Chapman and Dyer's supporters to help return the women to their expected social place.

The local authorities' response reinforced the societal idea that men made laws and enforced policy, and women relied on and benefited from men's protection. Dyer and Chapman, in effect, used a cultural belief of female powerlessness to gain power, making skillful use of all the resources available to them to compete with their husbands for the children. Lacking the authority to make and enforce laws themselves, they orchestrated the assistance of those who could. In effect, though they lacked authority, they did indeed exert power.

Mary Dyer and Eunice Chapman succeeded in stirring up the town of Enfield to come to their defense, thus matching the support their husbands received from the Shakers. Eunice in particular gained the support of authorities, since her claim to her children was backed by the New York legislature. This legitimacy provided the basis for Evans's initial offer to escort Chapman to the Enfield Shakers and Merrill's subsequent assistance.

Despite the power of the law, Eunice's custody was based on the children being in New York, not New Hampshire, and thus the local officials insisted on speaking to James Chapman, implicitly recognizing him as the head of the Chapman family whether within or without the Shaker village. And although the town sympathized with Mary Dyer, the authorities refused to interfere in her situation, and promised the Shakers they would make no attempt to take the Dyer children.

Unlike Chapman's petition, Dyer's 1817 petition to the New Hampshire legislature had not become law. Evans did not offer to escort Dyer to the village. On Mary's subsequent visit to the village, several women, not men, accompanied her. Nonetheless, the town of Enfield supported in spirit Dyer's quest to retrieve her children. Mary and Eunice's very public protest of Shaker treatment led several Enfield residents to petition the June 1818 session of the legislature for assistance. Their written complaint revealed the motivation for participation in the mob and indicates yet another breach in this multilayered social drama. This breach between townspeople and Shakers reinterprets the support some townspeople gave to Dyer and Chapman as abused women-without-children. Instead of supporting the mothers' claims against the Shakers, the petition concerned the outcome of the Shakers' failure to support such women: economic loss and disruption of the peace.

Joshua Stevens represented forty-seven Enfield residents when he requested that the legislature force the Shakers to provide for the non-Shaker wives and children of male converts. His concern was not really for the ill-treated women but rather for the residents of Enfield, who complained of frequent disturbances from women crying in the streets and going from door to door in search of help. This disruption of the town's peace was equally distressing to Shaker James Pettingill, who complained of Mary's "very high" tone and Eunice's "very haughty" behavior. Pettingill concluded that it was a pity "that the United States are so reduced as to be stirred up by two old women running up and down the streets" (Statement 1818). Both Pettingill and Stevens focused on the women's public display.

To Stevens and his petitioners, the recent mob illustrated the social disorder that resulted from the Shaker annulment of marriages, a long-standing anti-Shaker complaint. When Shakerism divided a family, vulnerable, pious women who refused to join the sect were left without their husbands' protection. This led to two problems. Some women, like Mary Dyer and Eunice Chapman, stepped into a public and vocal role disturbing the peace with their call to arms (e.g., Chapman's harangue in the street). Far from the domestic women early-nineteenth-century society revered, Shaker action forced a reversal of roles. Dyer and Chapman's public campaign breached gender norms. In addition to the disruption of expected gender roles, Stevens and others feared the village of Enfield would be forced to support the wives and children of Shaker husbands as the new town poor. By early-nineteenth-century law, a husband and wife were one legal identity, that of the husband. A married woman without her husband had no legal identity, and little social identity.

Without the support of their Shaker husbands and without the possibility of divorce (in 1818 New Hampshire), women would be destitute. As Stevens and his fellow townspeople recorded in their petition to the legislature, the Shaker society "by their conduct" were "disturbing the peace of the community at large." Women abandoned by Enfield Shaker husbands were "crying in the street and going from house to house mourning about their situation" (Dyer 1818, 34–35). The desire for social order and economic stability formed the heart of the Enfield residents' petition and their participation in the mob.

Outcome

The final phase of the social drama is an outcome, reorienting opposing constituencies into "reintegration" or to "the social recognition . . . of irreparable schism" (Turner 1974, 41). The mob represented a public performance of power. The local participants demonstrated their right, as they saw it, to define and enforce community standards of behavior. Local officials supported this belief by the lack of opposing action. Residents harassed the Shakers by presenting a large gathering, patrolling the community borders, and firing guns to keep the Shakers on edge. When the mob surrounded the village on Thursday evening, the Enfield residents dramatically demonstrated how their majority culture surrounded and superseded that of the isolated Shaker settlement.

The Shakers, Dyer and Chapman, and local residents all called upon the power of local officials for resolution. The Shakers' plea to Evans and Merrill to stop the mob illustrated that although living separately from the world, the Shakers saw themselves as tied to the world. They recognized the power of local law and law enforcement and indicated their willingness to consent to the law. In calling upon local officials, the Shakers asserted that as members of the wider community of the town of Enfield, they had the same rights to privacy, to religious freedom, and to protection from unlawful search as any non-Shaker and asked the local powers to uphold those rights.

Dyer and Chapman sought allies to use authority and power on their behalf. Local residents looked to authorities both for official support of their position and to look the other way during the mob's unorthodox village search. Merrill used his position to speak for the crowd and simultaneously to the crowd, controlling the potentially dangerous situation.

Although the mob at Enfield reached an outcome—reestablishment of a more or less peaceful relationship between the Shakers and the town of Enfield—the tension between the communal group and the host society remained. In 1828, two hundred petitioners (led by James Willis, the owner of the inn where the 1818 mob idea was hatched and in 1828 Enfield's representative to the legislature) complained to the New Hampshire legislature that the Enfield Shakers forced husbands to violate the marriage contract, taught husbands to hate their wives, and by presenting false information prevented children from making a rational decision whether to remain with the Shakers or leave. After a lengthy series of delays and extensions, the legislature dismissed the petition.

Both at Enfield and at other Shaker sites, flare-ups between Shakers and surrounding communities continued throughout the antebellum nineteenth century, each social drama highlighting tensions between changing societal norms and the communal experiment. The Shakers were not alone is such conflicts. Catholics and Mormons, too, would face crowd violence in social dramas of their own (Givens 1997; Schultz 2000).

The 1818 Enfield incident illustrated that mob actions are not chaotic acts of violence, but serve instead as meaningful social dramas that highlight shared values and ideals for participants. Further, as the mob event at Enfield indicated, the progression through a social drama was not linear, moving smoothly from one stage to the next. The action bounced between crisis and resolution for three days, with different segments of the heterogeneous mob finding the resolution at different points. This complicates Turner's model and suggests that the apparent unity of some social dramas masks a much more complex bundle of subgroups and sub-social dramas. The mob at Enfield was not simply the Shakers against the townspeople. Like individual fibers in a thick rope, the mob at Enfield social drama was composed of several social dramas moving to their own rhythms, yet understood collectively by participants as one event.

Blaisdell's admonition forced progression to an outcome, yet one that did little to eliminate entirely tensions between Shakers and the surrounding town. A close examination of these social dramas suggests that in the relationship between communal group and surrounding society, the breach is ever-present. In intentional communities, members have already breached a definition of expected residence patterns, marriage rules, or economic practices (among other social factors) in choosing an alternative living situation. Although some "cultural overlap" exists between the intentional community and the surrounding national culture, when the cultural overlap between intentional community and national community is strained, in conflict, or incompatible, the breach widens to crisis (Janzen 1981). The outcome Blaisdell achieved was restoration of the imaginary stability between town and Shakers who, it could be said, established as their norm an agreement to disagree. In between the communal group and the surrounding community is a borderland where certain practices, beliefs, or values may collide. Because of this difference, a breach seems to be an ever-present specter. Given particular individuals or historical circumstances, the breach is exacerbated, quickly leading to crisis.

Epilogue

Judge Blaisdell's admonition to the participants in the mob offered an effective resolution to the mob event. The Shakers forced the town to adhere to legal measures rather than violence to resolve conflicts. Despite this measure of success, the Shakers had indeed been caught in a lie regarding the whereabouts of the Chapman children. The following spring, Eunice returned to Enfield with a writ of habeas corpus and the Shakers dutifully released her daughters.

Mary Dyer placed her second petition before the New Hampshire legislature a month following the appearance of the mob. The petition was dismissed, but a legislative committee did take up the issue of divorce and several years later modified New Hampshire law to permit divorce in situations (such as that of the Dyers) when one spouse belonged to a sect that professed the marriage bond was void. On this basis, Mary received her divorce in 1829.

Having regained a legal and social identity, Mary (who returned to the use of her maiden name, Marshall), purchased a small house not far from the Enfield Shaker village, and there she continued to write anti-Shaker works and argue for the rights of mothers until her death in 1867. Her former husband and four of her five children remained Shakers until their deaths. Her middle child, Jerrub, apostatized from the Shakers in 1852, married a former Shaker woman, and emigrated to Wisconsin.

Notes

The author is grateful to the administrators of the Milton R. Sherman Collection and to Mary Ann Haagen for their generosity in sharing key resources. In addition, the author acknowledges the careful critique of this work offered by Cheryl Boots, Susan Love Brown, Candace Kanes, Jeanne Quinn, Peter Laipson, Rebecca Noel, and David Shawn.

1. It seems that Mary Dyer may have been working in the background while the Chapmans fought. James Chapman's arrest was based on Mary Dyer's charge of physical abuse. Dyer alleged that during one of her many attempts to visit the children, Chapman, who lived with Joseph Dyer at the North House, used excessive physical force to bodily remove Mary from the Shaker village. Perhaps this incident, which had occurred long before the mob event, was resurrected during the volatile evening as a means to remove James Chapman and force a resolution to the crisis. Whether Mary Dyer or local officials concocted this plan is unclear.

Reference List

Blake, Nelson. 1960. Eunice against the Shakers. *New York History* 41:359–78.

Brewer, Priscilla. 1986 *Shaker Communities, Shaker Lives.* Hanover, N.H.: University Press of New England.

Chapman, Eunice. 1817. *An Account of the People Called Shakers.* Albany, N.Y.: printed for the Authoress.

———. 1818. *No. 2 Being the Additional Account of the Conduct of the Shakers.* Albany, N.Y.: printed by I. W. Clark for the Authoress.

De Wolfe, Elizabeth A. 1996. *Erroneous Principles, Base Deceptions, and Pious Frauds: Anti-Shaker Writing, Mary Marshall Dyer, and the Public Theater of Apostasy*. Ph.D. diss., Boston University.

Dyer, Mary Marshall. 1818. *A Brief Statement of the Sufferings of Mary Dyer*. Concord, N.H.: printed by Joseph C. Spear.

———. 1822. *A Portraiture of Shakerism*. [Haverhill, N.H.]: printed for the Author.

———. 1847. *The Rise and Progress of the Serpent from the Garden of Eden, to Present Day.* Concord, N.H.: printed for the Author.

Gilje, Paul A. 1987. *The Road to Mobocracy: Popular Disorder In New York City, 1763–1834*. Chapel Hill: University of North Carolina Press for the Institute of Early American Culture.

Givens, Terryl L. 1997. *The Viper on the Hearth: Mormons, Myths, and the Construction of Heresy.* New York: Oxford University Press.

Humez, Jean M. 1994. A Woman Mighty to Pull You Down: Married Women's Rights and Female Anger in the Anti-Shaker Narratives of Eunice Chapman and Mary Marshall Dyer. *Journal of Women's History* 6:90–110.

Janzen, Donald E. 1981. The Intentional Community—National Community Interface: An Approach to the Study of Communal Societies. *Communal Societies* 1:37–42.

Johnson, Theodore E. 1969. *Life in the Christ Spirit*. Sabbathday Lake, Me.: United Society of Shakers.

Lyon, John. 1818. Statement of John Lyon. In *Historical Notes Having Reference to Believers at Enfield,* comp. Henry Blinn. Typescript. Shaker Library, Sabbathday Lake, Maine.

McNemar, Richard. 1819. *The Other Side of the Question*. Cincinnati: Looker, Reynolds, and Co.

Richards, Leonard L. 1970. *Gentlemen of Property and Standing: Anti-Abolition Mobs in Jacksonian America*. New York: Oxford University Press.

Rudé, George. 1981 *The Crowd in History: A Study of Popular Disturbances in France and England, 1730–1848*. London: Lawrence and Wishart.

Schultz, Nancy Lusignan. 2000. *Fire and Roses: The Burning of the Charlestown Convent, 1834*. New York: The Free Press.

A Statement concerning the Mob at Enfield. 1818. Ms. in The Milton R. Sherman Collection (Armonk, N.Y.).

Stein, Stephen. 1992. *The Shaker Experience in America*. New Haven: Yale University Press.

Turner, Victor. 1974. *Dramas, Fields, and Metaphors. Symbolic Action in Human Society*. Ithaca, N.Y.: Cornell University Press.

———. 1984. Liminality and the Performative Genres. In *Rite, Drama, Festival, Spectacle: Rehearsals toward a Theory of Cultural Performance,* edited by John K. MacAloon, 19–41. Philadelphia: Institute for the Study of Human Issues.

Van Vleet, Abram. 1818. *An Account of the Conduct of the Shakers, in the Case of Eunice Chapman and her Children.* Lebanon, Ohio: Van Vleet & Camron.

Weinbaum, Paul O. 1979. *Mobs and Demagogues: The New York Response to Collective Violence in the Early Nineteenth Century.* [Ann Arbor, Mich.]: UMI Research Press.

Woods, Robert L. 1983. Individuals in the Rioting Crowd: A New Approach. *Journal of Interdisciplinary History* 14:1–24.

7

Coming Together and Breaking Apart: Sociogenesis and Schismogenesis in Intentional Communities

Jonathan G. Andelson

I take "communal" to signify a sense of shared identity or fellowship felt by a group of people. The shared identity may be temporary or long-lasting, and it may be based on many markers or only a few. A "communal society," then, is a full-featured or institutionally complete ongoing social form in which the bonds connecting the members to one another and to the group as a whole are, whatever else they may be based on, based on feelings of fellowship. An "*intentional* communal society" (more commonly referred to as an intentional community) is one whose members actively strive to forge such a shared identity. It can be differentiated from the traditional community, whose origins are more often than not, as the saying goes, "lost in the mists of time," and the circumstantial community, whose members are thrown together by happenstance and may in fact develop little if any sense of shared identity. The term intentional community has generally been used to refer to such historical groups as the Shakers, the Amana Society, and the Oneida Community, and such contemporary communities as the Hutterites, the Israeli kibbutzim, and Findhorn in Scotland.

Besides having definable beginnings in most cases, the majority of intentional communities, after existing for varied lengths of time, experience decline and collapse. As a result, many studies of intentional communities have included an analysis of their rise and fall.[1] However, most previous studies have been particularistic rather than comparative and theoretical. While they offer explanations for the careers of individual communities, they avoid more comprehensive models and explanations. Those studies that do embrace nomothetic goals typically focus on either the origins of such communities (Berry 1992, chap. 2; Bainbridge and Stark 1979; Barkun 1984; Douglas 1969; Wallace 1956) or their demise (Latimore 1991), but usually not both together. One theoretical framework that does incorporate both beginnings and endings, at least implicitly, is Donald Pitzer's model of "developmental communalism"; this model, however, is exceedingly general and does not specify alternative pathways of change (1989).

The most influential theoretical approach in the study of the life cycle of intentional communities has been Kanter's work on "commitment" and the ways in which communitarian groups foster it (1972). The commitment concept, though at first seemingly processual, is treated by Kanter in quite static terms. One looks at a community, determines how many and what kinds of "commitment mechanisms" it has, and relates that to the issue of community longevity. The entire emphasis is on the structure and functioning of the community seen in a kind of suspended animation, independent of how and why the community formed, how and why it might have changed, or how and why it fell apart.

There are several problems with Kanter's approach. First is the question of intentionality on the part of the communitarians who "use" these mechanisms. While Kanter never claims that the leaders or members of a community adopt particular customs or practices in order to promote commitment, neither does she ask why a practice (say, income sharing or celibacy) is present, apparently assuming that the reason, let alone how the members feel about the practice, does not affect its impact. The historical record calls these assumptions into question.

Second, Kanter looks only at the *number* of commitment mechanisms in a community and fails to consider their strength. For example, she scores both the Shakers and the Amana Society as favoring celibacy, but whereas the Shakers required celibacy for full membership, in Amana it was only encouraged (and only about 15 percent of the members practiced it).

Third, Kanter's model does not allow her to deal with changes in custom during the course of a community's history. For instance, Kanter scores celibacy as present among both the Rappites and the Zoarites, yet the Zoarites abandoned celibacy a decade after their founding (Nordhoff 1960, 102), and the Rappites adopted it two years after theirs (Nordhoff 1960, 72). It is unlikely that these developments are functionally equivalent.

Finally, Kanter finds that communities that lasted more than twenty-five years had significantly more commitment mechanisms than those that lasted less than twenty-five years, but she fails to perform the more telling test of her hypothesis: whether the total number of commitment mechanisms actually correlated with community longevity. In short, not only is Kanter's approach not processual, it is strikingly undynamic and insensitive to local conditions.

Clearly, we must continue to work toward a more dynamic model of the life cycles of intentional communities—one that includes the periods of disequilibrium at either end of their life spans and one that can be integrated with structural and functional models of the middle period of relative equilibrium. A useful starting point in developing such a model can be found in the works of Arnold Van Gennep (1960) and Victor Turner (1969) on rites of passage. Following Van Gennep's lead, Turner identified three stages in a rite of passage: separation, limen (the state between one status and another), and reaggregation. If one were to examine the life cycles of intentional communities from the standpoint of the surrounding society, these same stages could be discerned: *separation* of the members of the intentional community from the wider society; the period of the community's existence (of variable duration) in which it or its members possess some of the qualities of *liminality* (or marginality) identified by Turner; and ultimately, when the community fails, a *reaggregation* of its members back into the wider society. Seen in this way, the period of liminality is inherently transitory (as in rites of passage), and reaggregation is inevitable.[2]

If, however, we adopt a community-centered view of a community's life cycle, the first and last stages in Turner's model undergo an inversion in meaning. In this view, the beginning of the community involves not so much a separation as a *joining together,* an act of aggregation among individuals who share a vision, while the third stage involves an *unraveling* of the bonds that were created when the community began and that held the members together. From a community perspective, the significance of the "middle stage" also shifts. Most intentional communities reject the notion that their existence is inevitably temporary and instead embrace a separate existence as the goal state. This view is not entirely incompatible with Turner's model, since the importance of shared identity for communitarians resonates with Turner's description of *communitas*, one of the defining characteristics of the liminal period. Turner considers communitas one of two "juxtaposed and alternating" models "for human interrelatedness":

> The first is of society as a structured, differentiated, and often hierarchical system of politico-legal-economic positions with many types of evaluation, separating men in terms of "more" or "less." The second, which emerges recognizably in the liminal period, is of society as an unstructured or rudimentarily structured and relatively undifferentiated *comitatus,* community, or even communion of equal individuals who submit together to the general authority of the ritual elders. (1969, 96)

While no one would argue that intentional communities, least of all the successful ones, are unstructured, the desire for communitas is certainly an important actuating factor in the creation of most, if not all, of them (see Kamau, this volume).

My purpose in this essay is to further the development of a nomothetic model of the life cycle of intentional communities. I take a community-centered rather than society-centered approach, in which the formation of an intentional community is seen more as an act of coming together than an act of separation, and in which the dissolution of an intentional community is seen more as a breaking apart than a reincorporation. I use the term "sociogenesis" to refer to the formation of a community through the joining together of individuals, and the term "schismogenesis" to refer to the breaking of the bonds that held them together. While I recognize the centrality of the period of structure and communitas in the middle of a community's life, my focus is on the periods of disequilibrium at the beginning and end of its existence.

Sociogenesis

Sociogenesis refers to the process by which individuals move from a condition of mutual unawareness or at most casual acquaintance to one of having an ongoing relationship with one another that entails mutual interests, concerns, and efforts.[3] The root "socio" denotes sociality, association, or society in a general sense. The root "genesis" denotes emergence, development, origins. Sociogenesis is a process rather than an event. It occurs over time, though not an indefinite length of time, since most relationships between or among individuals become defined as such within a matter of months rather than over years or decades. Ambiguity about *whether* a relationship exists becomes unsettling if it is protracted. On the other hand, the *nature* of the relationship is subject to slow change, and up to a point such an evolution is part of sociogenesis. We can speak of sociogenesis as long as a relationship is becoming more complex, developing more facets, or growing deeper.

A useful way to think about a relationship is in terms of social bonds. A given relationship may be based on a single link or connection. The connection between an employer and an employee, for example, is an economic one, but perhaps nothing more. However, it is possible that in time the two might develop bonds of friendship, of religion (they belong to the same church), or even kinship (the worker marries the boss's son). As the number and variety of bonds increase, the complexity of the relationship also increases. The proliferation of bonds between individuals—the sharing of more and more aspects of identity—is part of sociogenesis. If and when the relationship stabilizes, sociogenesis has ceased. Some relationships may of course continue to develop indefinitely, as long as the individuals are connected to one another, but the concept of sociogenesis does not imply this.

Sociogenesis is clearly a vital process in the life cycle of an intentional community: without it there simply would be no community. Initially it involves the joining together of like-minded people in a total living situation. In the extreme, there is a change in the relationships among a group of individuals from not knowing one another at all to feeling closely bonded, from anonymity to communitas. Of course, less dramatic changes can also signal the origin of a community, as when several friends decide to live together and share resources. The initial bonding can for convenience be called *primary sociogenesis* to set it apart from other types of sociogenesis that take place once the community has formed. One of these involves the extension of bonds to new members recruited from the outside. Another involves the socialization of the children of community members into the community. These postfounding processes can be designated *secondary sociogenesis*. The emphasis here will be on primary sociogenetic processes.

The analysis of sociogenesis will emphasize the *patterns of interaction* that result in the formation of bonds rather than the cognitive or affective characteristics of those who form them. Beliefs, values, and motives are of course involved, but the focus is on formal social processes.[4] Three primary sociogenetic processes have produced most intentional communities: (1) the growth of bonds out of the allegiance of each individual to a charismatic leader, (2) the growth of bonds derived from a shared commitment to, or at least interest in, an ideology or lifestyle, and (3) the growth of bonds out of preexisting, noncommunitarian connections among individuals.

First, many communities form through the agency of charismatic leadership. Here, bonds initially develop between a charismatic figure and individuals attracted to his or her person and message. These bonds are typically hierarchical (or vertical) in nature, the adherent submitting to the greater wisdom, power, or ability of the leader, oftentimes as to a parent. The process has been treated intelligently by Bord (1975), who discusses many of the factors in a leader's appeal, including the way in which the leader delivers his or her message, and by Couch (1989), who emphasizes the processual nature of charismatic relationships. The essence of the charismatic process entails an exceptional individual speaking about society's or the world's problems and presenting an attractive and plausible communitarian solution to them—attempting, in Couch's words, to intertwine "the articulation of discontents" with "new definitions of reality" (1989, 272).

Both historic and contemporary intentional communities are famous (sometimes infamous) for the charismatic figures who founded them.[5] However, for a community to achieve the kind of internal coherence that allows it to function as a social, economic, and political unit—and that allows it to survive the death of the charismatic leader (see Miller 1991)—leaders must also make followers bond to one another. In some cases, of course, followers might have prior connections with one another, in which case the leader may attempt to redefine these prior bonds within the new charismatic context. An especially clear example of this is found in the early years of Islam, when Mohammed began to emphasize that the religious bonds among his followers were to take precedence over prior bonds of kinship (Guillaume 1956, 41; Watt 1961, 58). It is common for leaders to encourage followers to think of themselves as a "brotherhood" and even to call one another "brother" and "sister." (In celibate communities the full behavioral implications of this terminology are accepted.) At the same time, prior bonds that interfere or compete with charismatic influence, including prior kinship bonds, often must be denied or sacrificed.

The ways in which charismatic leaders stimulate the formation of bonds among their followers—what Couch (1989, 272) calls "the formation of new solidarities"—have not been studied to the extent that the charismatic-influence processes have. We should not assume that bonding among followers is simply a "natural" outgrowth of the charismatic bonds, since there are cases in which the horizontal bonds never form, at least not to a degree sufficient to hold the community together (Robert Owen's New Harmony is an example). Presumably such things as the recruitment of members with similar backgrounds and interests, the pursuit of shared economic interests, and the observance of common rituals contribute to the formation of bonds among the members. With the addition of horizontal to vertical bonds, the process of *charismatic sociogenesis* is fully underway.

A second type of sociogenesis begins under the influence of a shared ideology rather than a charismatic leader. Although parallel in many ways to the first type, the social dynamic is rather different. An ideology—whether formulated by a particular individual, as in the case of Fourierism, or by several people, such as the current eco-village ideal—is "in the air." It is discussed, and people who find it appealing begin to find one another. They draw closer, and some eventually take the next logical step of trying to put the ideology into practice within a community. While this might seem comparable to enacting the vision of a charismatic leader, the obvious distinction is that social bonding here is not initiated in a hierarchical or vertical relationship but in a horizontal one. No exceptional person serves as a touchstone (except possibly in a distant and detached way, as the figure of Fourier did for American Fourierists [Guarneri 1991, 93ff.]), and no one is in a position to provide the ultimate "yea" or "nay." Under these circumstances, sociogenesis is likely to involve more tentativeness, more mutual negotiation, and (unless the ideology is exceptionally well defined) more fumbling than in the charismatic type. Let us call it *ideological sociogenesis*.

Examples of ideological sociogenesis can be found in both nineteenth- and twentieth-century intentional communities, large and small, "successful" and unsuccessful. The many mid-nineteenth-century Fourierist phalanxes, as mentioned, formed in this way, although a few of them also had founders/leaders with some charismatic influence. Toward the end of the century, the labor movement and Edward Bellamy's popular book, *Looking Backward*, stimulated hundreds of enthusiastic reformers to found dozens of socialistic communities, among them Ruskin in Tennessee. The principal prior connection among the far-flung future members of Ruskin appears to have been their subscription to J. A. Wayland's socialist weekly newspaper, *The Coming Nation*. In 1894, Wayland issued an invitation to all of his readers who earlier had made contributions toward the establishment of a socialist colony to join him in Tennessee and build the new community, which Wayland named Ruskin in honor of John Ruskin, the English social theorist (Egerton 1977, 66ff.).

A contemporary example of growth from common ideology is the community of Twin Oaks, founded in Virginia in 1967 under the influence of the utopian ideas of the psychologist B. F. Skinner, as set forth in his novel, *Walden Two*. The eight original members of Twin Oaks came together at a conference whose organizers hoped would promote the formation of "a real, rural Walden Two community" (Kinkade 1973, 26), and it did. Although over time the community gradually dropped virtually all the elements of Skinnerian behaviorism (Kinkade 1994), the ideology played a key role in bringing the early members together.

A third type of sociogenesis occurs when the members of a preexisting, comparatively narrowly defined group—for example, a club or a church—find it necessary or advantageous or merely desirable to intensify their relationship. This involves a mutual decision to increase the variety of bonds that unite them in the direction of a "full-featured" relationship. Of course, some members may not wish to move in this direction, and they withdraw from the group. The remainder increasingly embrace common purpose through, for example, coresidence, intermarriage, joint ritual, or community of goods.

A wide variety of causes may stimulate this development. If a group faces persecution and bonds more closely for mutual support and protection, or if it faces challenges associated with moving to a frontier, we might speak of *pragmatic sociogenesis*. Alternatively, the members might begin to feel that their original, narrower purpose implicitly carries the promise of a fuller commitment that they now want to fulfill. This is especially imaginable with religious bodies. Or they might think that their original mission can be engaged more thoroughly by living in a community. Suitable labels might be found for these cases as well, but all of these examples have in common the notion of an intensification of prior bonds. The general term *intensifying sociogenesis* is, therefore, appropriate.

An example of intensifying sociogenesis is seen in the beginnings of the Brook Farm community. In the 1830s, a number of New England intellectuals, among them Ralph Waldo Emerson, Margaret Fuller, and George and Sophia Ripley, began to articulate a new theological cum philosophical social vision that came to be known as Transcendentalism. Described variously as a movement, a group, and a social circle (Rose 1981, 93ff.), the Transcendentalists visited one another's homes, patronized the same bookshop in Concord, Massachusetts, attended the same lectures, and wrote reformist tracts. In 1841, the Ripleys founded a community at Brook Farm, situated nine miles from Boston, in the hopes, as George Ripley wrote in a letter to Emerson,

> to insure a more natural union between intellectual and manual labor than now exists; to combine the thinker and the worker, as far as possible, in the same individual; to guarantee the highest mental freedom, by providing all with labor, adapted to their tastes and talents, and securing to them the fruits of their industry; to do away with the necessity of menial services, by opening the benefits of education and the profits of labor to all; and thus to prepare a society of liberal, intelligent, and cultivated persons whose relations with each other would permit a more simple and wholesome life, than can be led amidst the pressure of our competitive institutions. (Quoted in Sams 1958, 6)

Between 1841 and 1844, thirty-two people became members of Brook Farm, nearly all drawn from the Boston-Concord transcendentalist circle (Rose 1981, 131ff.).

A quite different instance of intensifying sociogenesis is seen in the Community of True Inspiration, which formed two communal societies in the United States: at Ebenezer, New York (1843–64), and Amana, Iowa (1854–1932). From their origin in Germany in 1714 until coming to New York, the Inspirationists were a religious association whose members lived in villages and towns scattered across west-central and southwest Germany, Switzerland, and Alsace. Emigration was triggered by a divinely inspired decree as the Inspirationists faced increasing intolerance in Europe. The practical difficulties associated with paying the poorer members' passage to America and establishing themselves in their new home prompted the Inspirationists to settle in nucleated communities (rather than dispersed, as in Europe) and to adopt community of goods. At Ebenezer and Amana the ties of religion were reinforced by ties of propinquity, intermarriage, economic and political association, and cooperative child care, among others (Andelson 1985, 1995).

Sociogenesis, the progressive affiliation between two or more people, is a crucial early step in the life cycle of every intentional community. It can proceed in a variety of ways, three of which have been identified above in ideal typical form. These do not exhaust the range of possibilities, but they cover a significant number of actual cases. We now turn to the contrary process, *schismogenesis*.

Schismogenesis

Elements of a model of schismogenesis were worked out by Gregory Bateson many years ago (Bateson 1936). Bateson defined schismogenesis variously as "progressive differentiation" (1972, 68) or "progressive escalation" (1979, 105). The term describes any pattern of interaction that causes the bond that unites people to weaken and break. Or, as Norman Denzin has put it, "These systems of exchange destroy the very values on which interaction is initially built" (1984, 486). It is a process of progressive dissociation (to add my own gloss), or progressive conflict or contradiction (Denzin 1984, 485).

Schismogenesis does not describe the decline of all intentional communities. The term implies a breach between subgroups within a community, a true falling *apart*. Some communitarian groups simply seem to fade out of existence. They develop a stable structure that lacks only the ability to perpetuate itself. Life may be agreeable and harmonious, but the system is ineffective against the threat of attrition by death or defection, usually because it either cannot or will not recruit new members. Examples include Zoar, the Sanctificationists of Belton (Chmielewski 1993), and perhaps the Shakers. Although the question lies beyond the scope of this paper, we might want to ask what else characterizes communities that decline and come to an end, but not through schismogenetic processes.[6]

Other communities do experience internal conflict, typically along what Bainbridge and Stark call "lines of cleavage"—"subnetworks that existed prior to the outbreak of dispute" (1984, 101). Such conflict can produce schisms within the group between more or less overt factions. If the issue that divides them is not a vital one, or if the conflict is managed carefully, the factions may continue to coexist within the group. Andrews, in his general work on the Shakers, referred to the emergence in Shakerism of two factions, which he labeled liberal and conservative (1963, 232). Although in Andrews's opinion the division weakened the Shakers, it did not split them asunder. Similarly, the vegetarians and the meat-eaters at Twin Oaks appear to tolerate each other without serious conflict (Kinkade 1994, 117–19).

In other instances, schismogenesis results in the breakup of the original community, but with one or both factions surviving. The Rappites' experience with the impostor Count Maximilian de Leon is a case in point. De Leon wooed roughly one-third of them away from allegiance to Father Rapp and left Economy with them in 1832. The community survived this mass defection, although it was considerably weakened. Many of the defectors, after de Leon's death, joined Wilhelm Keil's community in Bethel, Missouri, and in that way maintained elements of their shared identity (Arndt 1965, 449ff., 517). Another group, the Icarians, underwent a series of schisms over doctrine and practice between 1849 and 1881, and each time two communities sprouted from the preexisting one (Sutton 1994).

Schismogenesis has also undermined communities entirely. Oneida (Foster 1988), Robert Owen's New Harmony (Bestor 1970), the Ferrer Colony (Veysey 1978, 77ff.), and Amana (Andelson 1981) are among those in which schismogenesis either caused the community to fall apart entirely, or caused it to abandon fundamental elements of its original ideology and structure in order to survive.

What patterns can be identified in how the bonds of community are disrupted? In both his original article and in later writings, Bateson identified two types of schismogenesis, which he called *symmetrical* and *complementary*. In symmetrical schismogenesis, "the individuals in two groups A and B have the same aspirations and same behavior patterns, but are differentiated in the orientation of these patterns" (Bateson 1972, 68). The more A exhibits a particular behavior, the more likely B is to respond by exhibiting the same behavior. Common examples of this occur in interactions that we could describe as competition, rivalry, or boasting. Complementary schismogenesis, on the other hand, occurs in "interactional sequences in which the interactions of A and B were different but mutually fitted each other (e.g. dominance-submission, exhibition-spectatorship, dependency-nurturance)" (Bateson 1979, 193). Bateson felt that all instances of factioning in social groups could be described as one or the other type of schismogenesis, or as some combination of them.

These terms help us toward a fuller understanding of the schisms that divided the communities named above. For example, in Owen's New Harmony several factions arose, each asserting that it alone had the correct plan for implementing Owen's vision. Owen's tolerance (or perhaps it was his acute uncertainty) led to the unusual result of each faction being allowed to establish its own subcommunity at different locations on New Harmony property. The claims of each group were matched by denunciations and counterassertions from the others. As if all this was not enough to weaken the members' sense of shared identity, Owen himself fell into schismogenetic interactions with two other influential members—his principal associate, William Maclure, and the anarchist Paul Brown—further undermining the bonds of the community until the whole dissolved in a swirl of symmetrical schismogenesis (Bestor 1970, 160ff.).

An example with elements of both symmetrical and complementary schismogenesis can be seen in one period of Bruderhof history. Organized in 1920 through the charismatic Eberhard Arnold, the Bruderhof movement had by the 1950s grown to seventeen hundred members in ten communities (hofs) in five countries (Oved 1996, 207). However, in the aftermath of World War II the membership found itself confronting a number of divisive issues, among them strict adherence to doctrine versus greater spontaneity, doctrinal purity versus syncretism, social outreach versus focus on inward concerns, and democratic versus authoritarian decision-making (Oved 1996, 215–16; Zablocki 1971, 100ff.). Factions began to form, and "the years 1959 to 1962 were the period of the great crisis. . . . [which] involved all of the hofs, lasted for more than three years, and radically and permanently changed the basic structure of the community" (Zablocki 1971, 98–99).

The schismogenesis thus began symmetrically, but unlike New Harmony, one faction, concentrated in one of the hofs and led by Heini Arnold (the son of Eberhard Arnold), came to dominate the situation. This group began "to carve out a hegemonic status for itself in the movement, defining many of the conflicts in terms of the difference between 'warm-hearted' (themselves) and 'cold-hearted' members" (Oved 1996, 215–16). In a striking turn of events, the "cold-hearted" members began to back down, to play a submissive role in response to Arnold's assertion of dominance. Rather than saving the situation, however, this strategy exposed the "cold-hearted" group to increasing domination by the Arnold faction, which in the end expelled many members and prodded others "into endless rounds of self-examination and confessions" (Zablocki 1971, 108). The complementary interaction of dominance and submissiveness so divided the Bruderhof that the two groups could not coexist. The number of hofs fell from nine to six, and six hundred members left or were sent away.

In Oneida, events went somewhat in reverse. The community had been founded and operated for some time on the basis of John Humphrey Noyes's preeminent position in it. Because Noyes was the member most advanced in spirituality, he wielded impressive power in the community—power that his followers responded to initially with submissiveness. Although, according to the theory of Perfectionism, Noyes and the other spiritually advanced members were to help the rest attain perfection, in practice a split developed between Noyes and his lieutenants, on one hand, and the "oppressed" members, on the other (Carden 1971, 99). However, this was not the split that ultimately rocked the community to its foundation.

Rather, a symmetrical schism developed between followers of Noyes and followers of James Towner, who challenged Noyes's authority on a variety of issues but especially on the issue of the sexual initiation of female members of the community. The result of the challenge was that Noyes fled the community and left the two factions to reach agreement on their own. This led to an attempt to reconcile the practice of complex marriage with the Townerites' wish for egalitarianism, an attempt that in Carden's opinion could not succeed. Reluctantly, the Oneidans decided to abandon complex marriage in order to save the community, only to find that the entire social structure had been based upon complex marriage. Shortly afterward, Oneida began the process of disbanding the communal character of its utopia.

Amana presents yet another schismogenetic pattern. There a hierarchical arrangement began to develop in the community between an elder-manager class and the rest of the members (Andelson 1981). Certain families assumed more and more of the power in the seven villages and more and more of the privileges. For a time, their assertions of authority were accepted submissively by other members in a pattern of (limited) complementary schismogenesis. But eventually a significant number of members came to the conclusion that the system had lost its legitimacy and either apostatized, thus ending the complementary pattern, or sought in a variety of ways to "get around the rules."

The latter behavior initiated a second schismogenetic pattern between those dedicated to upholding the rules and those dedicated to subverting them. The more the first group tried to enforce the rules, the more the second group developed clever ways around them, leading to, as Bateson has suggested is often the case in complementary patterns, progressive distortion of the relations between (and even the personalities of) the members of both groups. Mutual resentment and suspicion, coupled with (but actually in part responsible for) a serious economic crisis, finally led the members to vote to reorganize Amana in 1932, separating the religious from the business operation of the community, discontinuing common property, and creating a joint-stock corporation.

Once schismogenetic patterns in particular communities have been identified, attention can turn to the kinds of processes that might exist or be implemented in communities to prevent schismogenesis. Several general kinds of processes can be noted. First, a shared opposition to an external factor can effectively suppress internal dissension (Bateson 1972, 71). This was likely the case for the Inspirationists, for example, when they were debating community of goods shortly after establishing their first settlement at Ebenezer, New York. Their new and foreign environment was an implicit factor in overcoming opposition to the plan.

Second, Bateson suggested that complementary interaction may offset symmetrical schismogenetic tendencies, and that symmetrical interaction may offset complementary schismogenetic tendencies (1972, 71). How this kind of balance could be built into a community remains to be seen. A third possibility is seen in the case of the Hutterites. Here the community counteracts tensions building up within it through formal, planned schisms called "branching out," which result in the formation of new colonies (Hostetler and Huntington 1996, 50–54). This appears to be a way of limiting the harmfulness of schismogenesis by normalizing it and could even be said to constitute a third type, *routinized schismogenesis*. A survey of other intentional communities would probably turn up other solutions to the problems of schismogenesis.

CONCLUSION

This paper deals with the beginnings and endings of communitarian groups. Attention has been drawn recently to the difficulties of precisely ascertaining either the beginning or the end of many of these communities. The concepts of sociogenesis and schismogenesis help to reduce this problem, because of their applicability to gradual and complex processes of community formation and collapse. The merit of these concepts does not depend, the way Kanter's (1972) commitment model does, for example, on being able to specify the dates on which a community began and ended. Nor do they depend on identifying as "present" or "absent" traits that might wax and wane over the course of a community's existence.

In addition to being analytical concepts, sociogenesis and schismogenesis have practical applications. This is most apparent in the case of schismogenesis, for a knowledge of the forms it can take would alert contemporary communities to possible schismogenetic problems and allow them to take measures to counter them, informed by the successes and failures of past groups.

The typology of sociogenetic processes would also have practical benefits if it could be shown that a connection exists between the kind of sociogenesis that leads to the formation of an intentional community and the kind of schismogenesis that is likely to threaten it. Unfortunately, there does not seem to be a simple connection. Charismatic sociogenesis can be followed by either complementary or symmetrical schismogenesis, as in the Bruderhof or Rappite cases, respectively. Communities formed through ideological sociogenesis seem more prone to symmetrical schismogenesis than they are to the complementary type, although if one faction in a community manages to convince all members that it possesses the "correct" interpretation of the ideology, the latter can occur.

Intensifying sociogenesis could be less susceptible than the other types to fatal schismogenetic processes simply because of the longer association among members and the more gradual accretion of bonds. The Inspirationists' desire to preserve their community in 1932, even as they disassembled the communal system, suggests this, as does the lingering affection that Brook Farmers held for their community long after a disastrous fire sealed its financial doom.

These ideas await rigorous investigation and testing.

Notes

1. See, for example, Andelson 1981; Bainbridge 1984; Bestor 1970; Botscharow 1989; Carden 1971; Foster 1988; Guarneri 1991; Lemieux 1990; Robertson 1972; Sutton 1994.

2. This rite of passage model has also been applied to religious pilgrimages (Turner 1974; Myerhoff 1974) in which both participants and anthropologists emphasize the inherently temporary character of the middle, or liminal, period.

3. After developing the sociogenesis concept, I discovered that the entomologist and sociobiologist E. O. Wilson (1985, 1490) used the term *sociogenesis* to refer to stages in the life history of social insects. His definition is: "the procedures by which individuals undergo changes in caste, behavior, and physical location incident to colonial development." Wilson's usage is very restrictive. The etymology of the word suggests broader possibilities.

4. Several other researchers have examined the processual nature of bond formation. Lofland, Stark, and Bainbridge (Lofland and Stark 1965; Stark and Bainbridge 1985) have demonstrated the importance of previous interpersonal networks in conversion to cults and sects. Bowlby's research on "attachment theory" (1979), though focusing on dyadic bonding, approaches the subject in processual terms and might be applicable to sociogenetic processes. The articles in Kimberly, Miles, and associates (1980) dealing with the "organizational life cycle" are also relevant.

5. Among the better-known ones are Ephrata's Father Friedsam Gottrecht (Conrad Beissel) (Klein 1972; Tussing 1990), the Shaker's Mother Ann Lee (Brewer 1986), Father George Rapp of the Harmony Society (Arndt 1965), New Harmony's Robert Owen (Bestor 1970), Joseph Smith of the Latter-Day Saints (Brodie 1972), the Icarians' Etienne Cabet (Sutton 1994), Oneida's John

Humphrey Noyes (Thomas 1977), Fountain Grove's Thomas Lake Harris (Schneider and Lawton 1942), Eric Jansson of Bishop Hill (Elmen 1976), Peace Mission's Father Divine (Weisbrot 1983), The Farm's Stephen Gaskin, and Findhorn's Peter and Eileen Caddy.

6. As the rate of individual or familial defection from a community rises, the situation begins to resemble and even function like schismogenesis, since the defections are increasingly likely to be the result of structural features of the community rather than idiosyncratic ones.

Reference List

Andelson, Jonathan G. 1981. The Double-Bind and Social Change in Communal Amana. *Human Relations* 34, no. 2:111–25.

———. 1985. The Gift To Be Single: Celibacy and Religious Enthusiasm in the Community of True Inspiration. *Communal Societies* 5:1–32.

———. 1995. From the Wetterau to Ebenezer and Amana: A Demographic Profile of the Inspirationists in America. In *Emigration and Settlement Pattern of German Communities in North America,* edited by Eberhard Reichmann, LaVerne Rippley, and Joerg Nagler, 55–76. Indianapolis: Max Kade German American Center, Indiana University-Purdue University at Indianapolis.

Andrews, Edward Deming. 1963. *The People Called Shakers*. New York: Dover.

Arndt, Karl J. R. 1965. *George Rapp's Harmony Society, 1785–1847*. Philadelphia: University of Pennsylvania Press.

Bainbridge, William Sims, and Rodney Stark. 1979. Cult Formation: Three Compatible Models. *Sociological Analysis* 40:283–95.

———. 1984. The Decline of the Shakers: Evidence from the United States Census. *Communal Societies* 4:19–34.

Barkun, Michael. 1984. Communal Societies as Cyclical Phenomena. *Communal Societies* 4:35–48.

Bateson, Gregory. 1936. *Naven*. Palo Alto, Calif.: Stanford University Press.

———. 1972. Culture Contact and Schismogenesis. Reprinted in *Steps to an Ecology of Mind*. New York: Ballantine Books.

———. 1979. *Mind and Nature*. New York: E. P. Dutton.

Berry, Brian J. L. 1992. *America's Utopian Experiments: Communal Havens from Long-Wave Crises*. Hanover, N.H.: University Press of New England.

Bestor, Arthur. 1970. *Backwoods Utopias; The Sectarian Origins and the Owenite Phase of Communitarian Socialism in America, 1663–1829*. Philadelphia: University of Pennsylvania Press.

Bord, Richard J. 1975. Toward a Social-Psychological Theory of Charismatic Social Influence Processes. *Social Forces* 53:485–97.

Botscharow, Lucy Jayne. 1989. Disharmony in Utopia: Social Categories in Robert Owen's New Harmony. *Communal Societies* 9:76–90.

Bowlby, John. 1979. *The Making and Breaking of Affectional Bonds.* London: Tavistock Publications.

Brewer, Priscilla. 1986. *Shaker Communities, Shaker Lives.* Hanover, N.H.: University Press of New England.

Brodie, Fawn M. 1972. *No Man Knows My History: The Life of Joseph Smith.* 2d ed. New York: Alfred A. Knopf.

Carden, Maren Lockwood. 1971. *Oneida: Utopian Community to Modern Corporation.* New York: Harper and Row.

Chmielewski, Wendy E. 1993. Heaven on Earth: The Woman's Commonwealth, 1867–1983. In *Women in Spiritual and Communitarian Societies in the United States,* edited by Wendy E. Chmielewski, Louis J. Kern, and Marlyn Klee-Hartzell, 52–67. Syracuse, N.Y.: Syracuse University Press.

Couch, Carl J. 1989. From Hell to Utopia and Back to Hell: Charismatic Relationships. *Symbolic Interaction* 12, no. 2:265–79.

Denzin, Norma K. 1984. Toward a Phenomenology of Domestic, Family Violence. *American Journal of Sociology* 90, no. 3:483–508.

Douglas, Mary. 1969. Social Conditions of Enthusiasm and Heterodoxy. In *Proceedings of the 1969 Annual Spring Meeting of the American Ethnological Society,* edited by Robert F. Spencer. Seattle: University of Washington Press.

Egerton, John. 1977. *Visions of Utopia: Nashoba, Rugby, Ruskin, and the "New Communities" in Tennessee's Past.* Knoxville: University of Tennessee Press.

Elmen, Paul. 1976. *Wheat Flour Messiah: Eric Jansson of Bishop Hill.* Carbondale: Southern Illinois University Press.

Foster, Lawrence. 1988. The Rise and Fall of Utopia: The Oneida Community Crises of 1852 and 1879. *Communal Societies* 8:1–17.

Guarneri, Carl J. 1991. *The Utopian Alternative: Fourierism in Nineteenth-Century America.* Ithaca, N.Y.: Cornell University Press.

Guillaume, Alfred. 1956. *Islam.* Baltimore: Penguin Books.

Hostetler, John, and Gertrude Enders Huntington. 1996. *The Hutterites in North America.* Fort Worth, Tex.: Harcourt Brace College Publishers.

Kanter, Rosabeth Moss. 1972. *Commitment and Community: Communes and Utopias in Sociological Perspective.* Cambridge: Harvard University Press.

Kimberly, John R., Robert H. Miles, and associates. 1980. *The Organizational*

Life Cycle: Issues in the Creation, Transformation, and Decline of Organizations. San Francisco: Jossey-Bass.

Kinkade, Kathleen (Kat). 1973. *A Walden Two Experiment*. New York: William Morrow.

———. 1994. *Is It Utopia Yet? An Insider's View of Twin Oaks Community in Its Twenty-Sixth Year*. Louisa, Va.: Twin Oaks Publishing Company.

Klein, Walter C. 1972. *Johann Conrad Beissel: Mystic and Martinet, 1690–1768*. Philadelphia: Porcupine Press.

Latimore, James. 1991. Natural Limits on the Size and Duration of Utopian Communities. *Communal Societies* 11:34–61.

Lemieux, Christina M. 1990. The Sunrise Cooperative Farm Community: A Collectivist Utopian Experiment. *Communal Societies* 10:39–67.

Lofland, John, and Rodney Stark. 1965. Becoming a World-Saver: A Theory of Conversion to a Deviant Perspective. *American Sociological Review* 30:862–75.

Miller, Timothy. 1991. *When Prophets Die: The Postcharismatic Fate of New Religious Movements*. Albany: State University of New York Press.

Myerhoff, Barbara. 1974. *Peyote Hunt: The Sacred Journey of the Huichol Indians*. Ithaca, N.Y.: Cornell University Press.

Nordhoff, Charles. 1960. *The Communistic Societies of the United States*. New York: Hillary House Publishers.

Oved, Yaacov. 1996. *The Witness of the Brothers: A History of the Bruderhof*. New Brunswick, N.J.: Transaction.

Pitzer, Donald E. 1989. Developmental Communalism: An Alternative Approach to Communal Studies. In *Utopian Thought and Communal Experience,* edited by Dennis Hardy and Lorna Davidson. Enfield, England: Middlesex Polytechnic, School of Geography and Planning.

Robertson, Constance Noyes. 1972. *Oneida Community: The Breakup, 1876–1881*. Syracuse, N.Y.: Syracuse University Press.

Rose, Anne C. 1981. *Transcendentalism as a Social Movement, 1830–1850*. New Haven: Yale University Press.

Sams, Henry W. 1958. *Autobiography of Brook Farm*. Englewood Cliffs, N.J.: Prentice-Hall.

Schneider, Herbert W., and George Lawton. 1942. *A Prophet and a Pilgrim*. New York: Columbia University Press.

Stark, Rodney, and William Sims Bainbridge. 1985 *The Future of Religion*. Berkeley: University of California Press.

Sutton, Robert P. 1994. *Les Icariens: The Utopian Dream in Europe and America*. Urbana: University of Illinois Press.

Thomas, Robert David. 1977. *The Man Who Would Be Perfect: John*

Humphrey Noyes and the Utopian Impulse. Philadelphia: University of Pennsylvania Press

Turner, Victor. 1969. *The Ritual Process: Structure and Anti-Structure*. Chicago: Aldine.

———. 1974. *Dramas, Fields, and Metaphors: Symbolic Action in Human Society*. Ithaca, N.Y.: Cornell University Press.

Tussing, Ann K. U. 1990. The Hungry Orphan: Conrad Bessel. *Communal Societies* 10:87–101.

Van Gennep, Arnold. 1960. *The Rites of Passage*. Chicago: University of Chicago Press.

Veysey, Laurence. 1978. *The Communal Experience: Anarchist and Mystical Communities in Twentieth-Century America*. Chicago: University of Chicago Press.

Wallace, Anthony F. C. 1956. Revitalization Movements: Some Theoretical Considerations. *American Anthropologist* 58, no. 2:264–81.

Watt, W. Montgomery. 1961. *Islam and the Integration of Society*. Evanston, Ill.: Northwestern University Press.

Weisbrot, Robert. 1983. *Father Divine and the Struggle for Racial Equality.* Urbana: University of Illinois Press.

Wilson, E. O. 1985. The Sociogenesis of Insect Colonies. *Science* 228, no. 4707:1489–95.

Zablocki, Benjamin David. 1971. *The Joyful Community*. Baltimore: Penguin Books.

8

Community as Cultural Critique

Susan Love Brown

The distinction between community and society has a long history within social thought (see Tönnies 1957 and Durkheim 1984). But whereas some "communities" constituted societies themselves in the past, all communities in the world today exist within the context of larger societies. Communities constitute viable units for the study of state societies and are also a powerful means of integrating the individual and society and providing a focus for the study of change (see Brown 1987, 6–16 and Janzen 1981). Intentional communities—a product of state societies—are especially useful in this regard. In the interest of bringing Western state societies into the human continuum established by a century of anthropological study outside of the West, I analyze the formation of intentional communities as a variety of revitalization movement peculiar to state societies, as mentioned but left unexamined by Wallace in his original disquisition on the topic (1956).[1] In turn, I show that intentional communities as revitalization movements constitute an important form of cultural critique.

The idea of cultural critique entered the discipline of anthropology in 1986 by way of a book entitled *Anthropology as Cultural Critique* written by George Marcus and Michael Fischer, two anthropologists who explored the ethnographic enterprise as it then stood within the discipline. An approach usually identified with the Frankfurt School,[2] cultural critique arose in the 1980s as part of a reevaluation of the place of anthropology and its ethnographic method in a world within which western societies dominated other societies and in which a "crisis of representation" gripped this discipline. Anthropologists called upon themselves to account for the postcolonial and postmodern conditions in which people found themselves. Anthropologists were to use their knowledge of other societies "as a form of cultural critique for ourselves" (Marcus and Fischer 1986, 1).

The authors pointed out that cultural critique emerged from the works of both scholars and public intellectuals as "self-conscious criticism of the quality of life and thought in capitalist economies and mass liberal societies" (1986, 113). Two forms of cultural critique that characterized what Marcus and Fischer referred to as "contemporary" anthropology included "epistemological critique" and "cross-cultural juxtaposition," both meant to "defamiliarize," a strategy that forces us to view things differently. Epistemological critique entails "revising the way we normally think about things in order to come to grips with what in European terms are exotica" (1986, 138). The insights gained from studying outside the culture are brought back "to raise havoc with our settled ways of thinking and conceptualization" (1986, 138), presumably with the intention of advancing that thinking. Cross-cultural juxtaposition, on the other hand, involves the use of "substantive facts about another culture as a probe into the specific facts about a subject of criticism at home" (1986, 138).

Parallels to these forms of cultural critique originate in the revitalization process itself. The rise of revitalization movements in great numbers signals a disturbance in the larger society—that is, some respect in which the society has not met the needs of a substantial number of people. The form of the revitalization movement—whether it is religious or secular, whether it is based on the revival of a traditional culture, a new culture imported from outside the larger society, some mixture of traditional and new, or some as yet unrealized utopian goal (see Wallace 1956, 275)—often embodies the nature of the critique at hand and serves as a juxtaposition to the larger society. The contrast between the movement and the society at large casts the problem into specific relief and makes it evident, providing the opportunity for a reexamination. Epistemological critique comes later during "mazeway reformulation" (see Wallace 1956 and 1972) when new ways of looking and knowing emerge and solidify into doctrine, often from sources foreign to the culture in question.

For example, the emphasis of so many intentional communities on communal sharing in the utopian socialist period of communitarianism in the United States, 1824–48 (Zablocki 1980, 36–38) not only testified to the use of communalism as a survival technique but also constituted a critique of early capitalism and the inequalities that people assumed were a part of such an economic system. This was a period when the larger American society had begun to make the transition from an agrarian to an industrialized, urban society. It was during this period that Josiah Warren, credited as the first American anarchist, lived in Robert Owen's New Harmony community, an unsuccessful intentional community that lasted only two years (1825–27), faltering largely because of differences in social class, as well as general disorganization (Botscharow 1989, 76–90).

The New Harmony community itself served as a critique of capitalism and social and material inequality. For example, Josiah Warren believed that inequities among human beings were the result of the failure of labor to be properly rewarded:

> The most elegant and costly houses, coaches, clothing, food, and luxuries of all kinds are in the hands of those who never made either of them, nor ever did any useful thing for themselves or for society; while those who made all, and maintained themselves at the same time, are shivering in miserable homes, or pining in prisons or poor-houses, or starving in the streets. . . . At this point, society must attend to the rights of labor, and settle, once for all, the great problem of its just reward. This appears to demand a discrimination, a *disconnection,* a DISUNION between COST and *Value.* (Warren 1852, 41; emphases in original)

But Warren's distasteful experience at New Harmony allowed him to formulate a critique of communalism as well:

> It seemed that the difference of opinion, tastes and purposes *increased* just in proportion to the demand for conformity. Two years were worn out in this way; at the end of which, I believe that not more than three persons had the least hope of success. Most of the experimenters left in despair of all reforms, and conservatism felt itself confirmed. We had tried every conceivable form of organization and government. We had a world in miniature. We had enacted the French revolution over again with despairing hearts instead of corpses as a result. . . . It appeared that it was nature's own inherent law of diversity that had conquered us . . . our "united interests" were directly at war with the individualities of persons and circumstances and the instinct of self-preservation . . . and it was evident that just in proportion to the contact of persons or interests, so are concessions and compromises indispensable. (Warren, cited in Martin 1970, 9–10)

Warren, who was a printer, a musician, and an entrepreneur at heart, did not despair, however. He went on to become involved in three other intentional communities (Equity, Utopia, and Modern Times), this time fashioning them along anarchist lines with complete respect for the sovereignty of individuals (see Martin 1970 and Wunderlich 1986 and 1992 for accounts of these communities). Each of these experiments constituted a critique of some element of the larger society with which Warren and his fellow communitarians were dissatisfied. Warren wrote down his ideas based on his experiences, thus formulating a critique that served as a basis for the individualist anarchist movement that arose in his wake (Martin 1970). This critique called attention to both the need for political and economic reform and the need to respect the sovereignty of individuals.

In a different time and place, in 1942 (*not* a period of intense communitarianism in the United States), the founding of Koinonia Farm by Clarence Leonard Jordan and Martin England, two white Baptist ministers, constituted a radical, Southern, liberal critique of the racial segregation and the economic plight of African Americans, as well as of the gradualist policy of other liberal white Southerners in the larger society of the South. Liberal among liberals, Jordan and England "rejected the southern white liberals' reliance on gradual reform through legislative and court action. Instead, they pursued better relations through economic cooperation and building an interracial community where whites and blacks would live and work together" (K'Meyer 1997, 5). K'Meyer further notes:

> Koinonia Farm was an attempt to build the beloved community. Koinonians shared that goal with the civil rights movement, as they also shared a religious basis and a belief in nonviolence. For Koinonians this meant tearing down the walls that separated people and making everyone a part of God's family. They sought to achieve that by bringing whites and blacks together in work, through cooperation and equalized economic conditions. Koinonians also sought to foster spiritual sharing through common worship and informal fellowship. Finally, at the farm whites and blacks would simply live together. . . . (1997, 6)

Koinonia Farm constituted a major critique of Southern segregation and mistreatment of blacks, and it was in line with integrationist civil rights sentiments that arose, although it never really succeeded in accomplishing its goal (see Lee 1971). In time, its critique would be validated by the changes won by civil rights activists.

At the base of revitalization is the concept of change based on conscious critique. Wallace defines a revitalization movement as "a deliberate, organized, conscious effort by members of a society to construct a more satisfying culture" and designates it as "a special kind of culture change phenomenon" (1956, 265). These movements differ from other kinds of culture change, according to Wallace, because they are the product of "deliberate intent by members of a society" and result from the individual's decision to change his mazeway, or "mental image of society and its culture," in response to inordinate stresses in "an attempt to reduce the stress" (1956, 265-66). According to Wallace, individuals under such stress often seek to "make changes in the 'real' system in order to bring mazeway and 'reality' into congruence" (Wallace 1956, 265).

Wallace clearly saw revitalization as a response to psychic distress (1956, 266–67), but the response was conscious and intentional. Thus, movements toward revitalization necessarily constitute critiques of the societies in which they arise. Complex societies, especially those moving away from an agrarian basis toward an industrial one, generate psychic discontent on a regular basis, as testified to by the writings of social commentators on the problems of alienation and anomie and the studied analyses of capitalism and its discontents.

In this paper I bring together these two different concepts—revitalization and cultural critique—to understand the way in which people in state societies not only respond to change but through those responses critique their own societies and sometimes change them. Revitalization movements constitute indigenous forms of cultural critique in state societies, often separate from the critiques of scholars and public intellectuals but not unrelated to or unnoticed by them. Thus, revitalization constitutes a nonelitist form of critique available to the privileged and unprivileged alike.

Critiquing with One's Feet: The Intentional Community as Revitalization Movement

Intentional communities can be found in state societies all over the world and go back into ancient times in both the East and the West (Zablocki 1980, 20–31). Their enormously wide distribution marks them as a common social phenomenon in complex societies, springing from a common need to adjust to changes in the environment. The United States was the focus of much communitarian activity, even before the American Revolution. Intentional communities in the United States are older than the nation itself (Oved 1993, 3–4; Zablocki 1980, 33–35).

In the five distinct periods of communitarianism in the United States delineated by Zablocki (1980, 33–80), we can see that certain patterns of origin prevailed. Most of these communities came into being in reaction to stresses within the larger environment of Europe from which many fled. In the beginning (1620–1776), those who came and founded communities might be called religious dissenters who fled societies in which their beliefs made them vulnerable to reprisal. The Plymouth colony, the Amish, and the Shakers all fit into this category. They came to colonial America, where they believed tolerance was more easily observed and land was more readily available.[3]

Although people did form communities at many different times, the periods identified by Zablocki represented the clustering of community building set off by some special circumstance. If we examine the five phases of revitalization movements that Wallace delineates, presented below, we find that U.S. communitarianism fits within the pattern. To illustrate, I draw upon the latest instance of communitarianism—that which arose from 1965 to 1975—and an example from my own fieldwork at Ananda Village, a cooperative religious community in northern California founded in 1967 (Brown 1987).[4] Ananda and its founding illustrates how critique is inherent in revitalization and springs forth as new communities come into being.

Steady State (1946–59)

Communitarianism is not usually an outstanding feature in the landscape of state societies when things are operating in a relatively stable way. "For the vast majority of the population, culturally recognized techniques for satisfying needs operate with such efficiency that chronic stress within the system varies within tolerable limits" (Wallace 1956, 268). When this is the case, those individuals, who would be relatively few in number, might nevertheless find revitalistic alternatives, but these activities will not constitute a "mass" pursuit of new ways of coming to terms with stress.

Such was the case in the United States following World War II. Although the nation had suffered a severe depression in 1929 and found itself strained under the demands of warfare, the outcome of the war was favorable, and the United States emerged as a world leader in both politics and industry. Children were born at an unprecedented rate following the war, and with the growth of the American middle class from 13 percent of the total population to 46 percent of the total population, the country entered an era of unprecedented affluence and well-being (Strickland and Ambrose 1985, 533). This was the era of the rise of corporate America, the move to suburbia, and the child-centered society that produced unprecedented consumer goods, including the soon to be ubiquitous television.

Yet beneath the surface of this prosperity lurked social problems that would come to the fore in the fifties and sixties, leading to changes in American culture that can only be deemed radical. Besides the fear of atomic war that loomed since the bombing of Nagasaki and Hiroshima and the beginnings of the Cold War with the Communist world, and along with it McCarthyism, there was knowledge of the Holocaust and the beginning of the Civil Rights movement to secure the rights of black Americans. Eventually every group that sought rights within American society (women, Native Americans, Mexican Americans, the elderly, the disabled, and so on) joined in the critique of American society set in motion by members of the Silent Generation but carried by the Baby Boomer Generation (see Cleçak 1983).

A powerful critique of American society in the fifties can be found in the work of sociologists of the period, who authored such books as *The Lonely Crowd* (Riesman, Glazer, and Denney 1950) and *The Organization Man* (Whyte 1956). Intellectuals did not like what they saw as the conformity of the day, which they associated with changes in the way of doing business, especially with the rise of the corporation and the consumer society, an inevitable byproduct of America's great affluence. This period was also subjected to a powerful critique from artists in the form of the Beat Poets, whose unorthodox subject matter and public performance attested to the negative undercurrents of American life (see Gitlin 1987, 11–77).

During this postwar period, a young man named James Donald Walters (later to be known as Swami Kriyananda), an American raised in Rumania and educated in Switzerland, discovered his purpose in life after reading *Autobiography of a Yogi* by Paramahansa Yogananda (1985), the founder of the Self-Realization Fellowship (SRF) and the last of a line of gurus practicing kriya yoga. Yogananda had come to the United States in 1920 to attend the International Congress of Religious Liberals and had ended up making the United States his home and founding his own church meant to "destroy forever narrow divisions in the houses of God" (1985, 14; see also Brown 1987, 17–25).

From 1948 until 1962, Walters served as a monk of the Self-Realization Fellowship, becoming Brother Kriyananda in 1955 and making his first visit to India in 1958. He eventually became a member of the board of directors and a vice-president of SRF, and was initiated into the swami order in India, gaining the title of Swami Kriyananda. Yogananda, who would be a lifelong inspiration to Kriyananda, died in 1952 without ever instituting one of his lifelong dreams, world brotherhood communities. It was this particular part of Yogananda's program that Kriyananda would later take up when he founded his own community, Ananda Village. Kriyananda's years as a direct disciple of Yogananda, his experience within the Self-Realization Fellowship organization, and his experience in India would give him the credibility needed to establish one of the most successful of the intentional communities arising in the sixties. That experience was gained during this period of steady state in the United States.

The Period of Increased Individual Stress (1960–64)

Wallace states that this phase of revitalization is typified by the decrease in a society's "efficiency in satisfying needs" and the inability of individuals to relieve stress from the environment in the usual ways (1956, 269). In the United States, the negative undercurrents of American culture mentioned above did not go away. The great unifying element of television and mass culture (this was the era of *Life*, *Look*, and *Time* and the era of epic Hollywood films) had projected onto Americans an image of themselves that is easily captured in the slogan of the television show *Superman:* "Truth, Justice, and the American way."

Americans thought they could solve any problem with optimism, individual ingenuity, and hard work. The great generation of middle-class baby boomers born after the war (beginning in 1946), who came of age as an extremely idealistic generation because of these lessons (formal and informal), was thrust into the real world with a vengeance as they began to come of age in the sixties (see Brown 1992 and 1999). Through the magic of television, boomers witnessed the battle of nonviolently protesting blacks in the South for the very rights that were to be guaranteed to every citizen.[5] These battles, which had begun in 1955 with the Montgomery Bus Boycott, erupted into the student population with the first sit-in at Woolworth's by students in Greensboro, North Carolina, in 1960. The images of young, black schoolchildren attempting to enter previously segregated white schools, surrounded by jeering crowds, police officers, and dogs straining at the bit, were stamped indelibly on the minds of vanguard boomers and made them question the values of American life.

These battles spilled over into the political arena as Southern blacks in the Democratic Party began to vie for convention seats against Southern whites in 1964, and as blacks attempted to enter institutions from which they had been barred on the basis of color alone. Peaceful protests generated violent reactions, indicating struggles for change that not all Americans were ready to embrace. The failure of American society to make real the ideals that boomers had been taught struck them as hypocrisy.

Boomers also became politically aware through the first televised presidential debate between Richard M. Nixon and John F. Kennedy in 1960. Kennedy was inaugurated in 1961, and shortly afterward the international situation escalated, bringing the Soviet Union (headed by Nikita Khrushchev) head to head with the United States in the Cuban Missile Crisis in 1962 and creating the very real possibility of nuclear annihilation. By 1963 Americans had been exposed to an unprecedented amount of national violence: the murder of civil rights leader Medgar Evers in Mississippi, the Sunday bombing of a church in Birmingham, Alabama, that killed four young girls, and the assassination of President Kennedy and his alleged assassin in full view of all Americans because of the television coverage.

In 1962 Swami Kriyananda faced his own individual stress when he was asked to leave Self-Realization Fellowship,[6] which meant being cast out into the secular world just as it was about to go crazy. Kriyananda describes this period as "the bleakest of my life," though he also acknowledges that

> abandoned as I felt by God and man, I experienced, on some deep level within me, a subtle joy that never left me. . . . Though my present focus was on what to do with my life, and on the pain that attended that problem, at the same time, and within the same range of vision—closer, however, and therefore

> blurred—was this joy. Dimly I could perceive its outlines, while its presence somehow eluded me. (1977, 588)

During this time he lectured in two different venues: the American Academy of Asian Studies, where he was invited by Dr. Haridas Chaudhuri to lecture on raja yoga (Kriyananda 1977, 591), and the Cultural Integration Fellowship in San Francisco (Nordquist 1978, 28). Kriyananda was strategically placed to take advantage of the new interest that arose in Eastern religions in the coming period of cultural distortion, because of his familiarity with India and yoga. An interest in Eastern ideas would become a vital part of the growing spirituality that later became known as the New Age movement. The tradition of turning to the East at particular times in American history would be taken up again during the sixties (see Diem and Lewis 1992 and Ellwood 1992).

The Period of Cultural Distortion (1965–69)

"In this phase," says Wallace, "the culture is internally distorted; the elements are not harmoniously related but are mutually inconsistent and interfering. For this reason alone, stress continues to rise" (1956, 269). With the continued rise of stress, greater and greater distortions of the culture occur, leading to more stress and finally to apathy. It is in this phase of American history that "dropping out" became the call of the day for some boomers, and the counterculture arose for those who did not think it worth their while to engage in politics any longer. The sexual liberation made possible by the approval of the birth control pill in 1960 had also ushered in another period of "free love," openly challenging the sexual mores of the parental generation. The "generation gap" arose as other boomers insisted on trying to implement the values their parents had taught them, but with an eye toward reconciling the gap between the real and the ideal, which had caused the crisis in the first place.

These boomers and their older brothers and sisters joined in the Civil Rights movement and campus protests over the Vietnam War. Former Black Muslim leader Malcolm X was assassinated in February 1965. The year 1965 also signaled the beginning of massive war protests due to the immediate threat to the lives of male boomers themselves.

> Between 1964 and 1965, the months immediately after the Tonkin Gulf resolution, the number of draft-eligible 18-year-olds went up faster than at any time in the nation's history. In 1964 the pool of draftable 18-year-old men was 1.4 million; a year later it had jumped 35 percent to 1.9 million. By July 1, 1965, the overall draft reservoir was one-third larger than in 1963. . . . Then, immediately after the number of 18-year-olds peaked in the middle of 1965, the Vietnam draft calls began. (Jones 1980, 106–7)

As protest and draft resistance grew, the other problems of the nation did not subside. Instead, they seemed to grow worse. In fact, the United States evidenced all of the "precipitators of rebellion and revolution" as stipulated by William Haviland (1997, 714): the "establishment" had lost credibility with a large proportion of the population, primarily because political and religious leaders did not act decisively to end injustices; the government was indecisive and its leaders lost the support of the intellectuals, especially with regard to its subterfuge in matters pertaining to Vietnam; and charismatic leaders rose up and mobilized citizens in a number of movements both social and political involving everyone from folk and rock singers to political leaders. The only factor not present was "the threat to recent economic development." (This would come later in the seventies after the withdrawal from Vietnam and an economic downturn that ended the period of communitarianism.) Indeed, a cultural revolution *was* taking place.

Further distortion occurred and reached its peak in 1968 when Martin Luther King Jr. was assassinated in April and Senator Robert F. Kennedy in June. Then the trouble was compounded by the confrontation at the Democratic convention in Chicago between student radicals and the Chicago police. The psychic equilibrium of many Americans was completely upset by the sweeping changes and what appeared to be a society falling apart.

Revitalization movements in the form of a rapidly growing communitarianism and new religious movements began almost simultaneously with the period of distortion.

The Period of Revitalization (1965–75)

As increasing distortion threatens dire consequences for a society (Wallace 1956, 270), it is not unusual for people to attempt to regain their psychic equilibrium through the formation of new religions, crisis cults, or even intentional communities. Out of the distortion of the sixties, then, grew many kinds of revitalization movements, including an unprecedented period of community building in the United States (Zablocki 1980, 34, 41–80).

In his book *Getting Saved from the Sixties*, Steven Tipton argues that "Sixties youth have joined alternative religious movements basically . . . to make moral sense of their lives" (1982, xiii). According to Tipton, problems arose from "the delegitimation of utilitarian culture, and with it the stripping away of moral authority from major American social institutions" (1982, 29). He further notes:

> In the atmosphere of disappointment and depression that followed the conflicts and failures of the sixties, many youths sought out alternative religious movements. Disoriented by drugs, embittered by politics, disillusioned by the apparent worthlessness of work and the transiency of love, they have found a way back through these movements, a way to get along with conventional American society and to cope with the demands of their own maturing lives. For some youths the social and ideological stability of these movements has meant psychological and even physical survival. (Tipton 1982, 30)

This "revitalistic" response that Tipton describes accounts for the founding of Ananda Cooperative Village by Swami Kriyananda in the period 1967–69. Kriyananda, previously cast adrift from the Self-Realization Fellowship but continuing to teach yoga in the northern California area as interest in these teachings increased, was poised at the precise moment in history when these practices and ideas were enjoying a rebirth within American culture. Ananda Cooperative Village was founded at this time, and its early years and subsequent growth are recorded below in such a way as to demonstrate just how Ananda fits into the revitalistic pattern.

According to Wallace, there are "six major tasks" that revitalization movements must perform.

(1) Mazeway reformulation. "[T[he reformulation of the mazeway generally seems to depend on a restructuring of elements and subsystems which have already attained currency in the society and may even be in use, and which are known to the person who is to become the prophet or leader" (Wallace 1956, 270). In the case of Ananda, its religious elements had long been a part of American culture and would become a part of what eventually became known as New Age religion (Alexander 1992; Brown 1992).

Americans have had a long history of interest in religions from the East (see Diem and Lewis 1992; Ellwood 1992; Jackson 1981; and Thomas 1930). Thomas Jefferson, John Adams, Benjamin Franklin, and Henry David Thoreau had all shown an interest in eastern ideas at one time. As mentioned, Yogananda himself originally came to the United States in 1920 to attend the International Congress of Religious Liberals. He founded the Self-Realization Fellowship in Los Angeles, a church that has sustained itself to this day. So the elements associated with yoga—meditation and the guru-disciple relationship—were familiar already within the American cultural milieu.

The more recent fascination of young people in the United States with Eastern religions could be traced to several factors: (1) the East represented an influence that was not-West and, therefore, constituted a novelty; (2) techniques of meditation produced the altered states of consciousness that many young people had experienced after taking hallucinogenic drugs; (3) Eastern religions did not possess the stigma of hypocrisy perceived by young people to be part and parcel of American religion.

Zablocki has pointed out that 96.4 percent of those living in communities derived from Eastern religions had used drugs before joining, compared to 56.2 percent of those joining Christian-based communities. Indeed, others have pointed out similar affinities between drug use, Eastern religious practices, and intentional communities (see Brown 1992 and 2001; Nordquist 1978; Robbins 1969).

Beyond this obvious appeal lay the ability of Yogananda's particular religious doctrine to help young people reconcile the many contradictions between cultural expectations and their personal values and experiences. Self-Realization provided a new way to meld the East and the West, science and intuition, individualism and communalism, altruism and self-interest—the basic conflicts confronting people in American society (see Brown 2001). This it accomplished through the practice of kriya yoga, a form of raja yoga in which people achieved union through meditation.

(2) Communication. According to Wallace, the leader who emerges to found the revitalization movement "becomes a prophet. The doctrinal and behavioral injunctions which he preaches carry two fundamental motifs: that the convert will come under the care and protection of certain supernatural beings; and that both he and his society will benefit materially from an identification with some definable new cultural system . . ." (1956, 273).

Swami Kriyananda, whose reputation as a direct disciple of Yogananda and respected teacher of yoga was growing in northern California, was already well entrenched in the tradition of the elements that suddenly became important components in the restructuring of worldview that occurred among young people in the sixties. Through his lecturing, he exposed more and more people to Self-Realization and the path of kriya yoga. Through his publication of *The Path: Autobiography of a Western Yogi* (1977), he consolidated this communication.

According to Nordquist, Kriyananda acquired the land that was to become Ananda Cooperative Village in 1967:

> One thing led to another and in a matter of months Kriyananda was co-owner of a beautiful tract of 172 acres in the foothills of the Sierra Nevada Mountains, near Nevada City, California. The legal ownership of this land was held by the Bald Mountain Association, a group consisting of Swami Kriyananda, Dick Baker, and the poets Gary Snyder and Allen Ginsberg. . . . The money for this venture was obtained by appeal to friends and through his yoga classes. The mortgage was high, 2,500 dollars per month, but by the end of the year most of the debt was paid off. Ananda Cooperative Village was under way (Nordquist 1978, 28–29)

Ananda Village at first was simply a refuge for Kriyananda and those who, like him, merely wanted a quiet place in the country as background for the meditation that was a major part of their lives. Kriyananda built his first home, a geodesic dome, and other buildings at the meditation retreat with money he raised through teaching yoga (Nordquist 1978, 29).

(3) Organization. What began as a meditation retreat with a few members in residence turned into a full-fledged community in 1969 when more land was purchased. Nordquist reports (1978, 30):

> [T]he need to find enough room for the increasing number of Ananda families to raise their children (at a distance from those attempting meditation) led to the purchase in 1969 of an additional 236 acres of land, including a farm approximately six miles from the Meditation Retreat.
>
> With the purchase of the Ananda Farm land, the development of Ananda Cooperative Village took its first major step towards self-sufficiency. But is [*sic*] was not an easy step, and the road towards the fulfillment of Kriyananda's ideals was to be as bumpy and difficult as the dirt roads of Ananda Farm.

Through word of mouth and a few well-placed articles about the community, the knowledge of Ananda's existence spread, and people began to arrive at the community in large numbers. One member recounted to Nordquist (1978, 32–33) how the growing number of people at Ananda split into two groups—those interested in yoga and meditation and those who were not. In late 1969, those who were casual visitors and not interested in yoga left. Kriyananda and other members committed to the community worked to reduce the debt that had accumulated, and they eventually worked out a plan. In the end, Ananda became a yogic community, organized as a village community and adopting a cooperative rather than a communal economic arrangement (Nordquist 1978, 33). Thus, Ananda Cooperative Village was born.

During an interview in 1986, Kriyananda described how his role in the community had changed over the years:

> Well, in the beginning the people who came were, by and large, not students of mine that had come to my classes—therefore,

> not people who had any particular dedication to fulfilling my dream that I had in founding the community. And I had a great deal of opposition from people, such that anything I proposed often would be opposed. Now, that's not the case. I find that people realize that I am a man of good will and also a man of vision and not a man who imposes on them but tries to help them to achieve what they're trying to achieve. And, as a result, we have a lot of harmony and no conflict of that sort, so it's gratifying to me on many levels. . . . It was very hard in the beginning, and now it isn't hard that way at all. (Kriyananda 1986)

By 1986 when I visited Ananda, Kriyananda was no longer involved in the day-to-day operations of the community. Others made decisions regarding maintenance, planning, and finances. Kriyananda was often away from the community or in seclusion. However, he had been elected spiritual director for life and oversaw the general welfare of the community with an informal council made up of the community managers, community ministers, and longtime members. This informal council oversaw the schools, centers, finances, and Ananda businesses.

Ananda Village, Inc., a nonprofit business that pays taxes, constituted the village government, which was run by a council and its committees. This council oversaw all of the day-to-day activities of the community, such as housing, firefighting, village gardens, and so on. The Ananda Church, the Fellowship of Inner Communion (formerly and in 1986 still legally the Yoga Fellowship), was a nonprofit, tax-exempt organization and separate legal entity run by Kriyananda and a board of senior disciples and those who had been members at least five years. The church oversaw Ananda's outreach facility, the Expanding Light, and Ananda publications.

The success of the community could also be attributed to its successful business enterprises, which provided income and jobs for many of its members. Other members held jobs outside of the community and ran their own businesses.

(4) Adaptation. Because revitalization movements are almost always perceived as unusual (and even threatening) by those in the larger society, they "almost inevitably will encounter some resistance"

(Wallace 1956, 274). This leads to the necessity of adaptation. The constant "reworking" of doctrine in response to experience and sometimes resistance often leads to "a better 'fit' to the population's cultural and personality patterns, and may take account of the changes occurring in the general milieu" (1956, 275).

The history of Ananda Village has been a history of adaptation to experience. Beginning with the original sorting out of members from those only passing through to the adoption of yoga as the central point of the community, Ananda has passed through many phases, some of which were responses to immediate crises and experience, and others of which were responses to the larger cultural environment in the United States.

Self-Realization became the central focus of the community rather early, and Paramahansa Yogananda became the community's guru, the last in a long line of gurus. Anyone joining Ananda had to accept Yogananda as his or her guru and follow the path of kriya yoga. Almost all of the people in the community are vegetarians, although this is not required, and the community functioned with only two formal rules at the time of my visit: no drugs (including alcohol) and no dogs.[7]

The community managers told me that visitors to Ananda were often taken by the strong feelings of community that they experienced while there. In order to avoid taking in members who were not serious about the spiritual commitment that came along with membership, a membership process developed that required potential memberships to learn about and work in the community before making a commitment to it.

Although Ananda originally experimented with communalism, people quickly realized that it wasn't going to work. Instead, members adopted a cooperative mode of operation in which members were encouraged to be both self-supporting and to contribute to the community. Many members started their own businesses, while others helped make Ananda-owned businesses successful. In 1986, Ananda owned a general store, a successful vegetarian restaurant and boutique in Nevada City, and the world's second-largest New Age bookstore in Menlo Park, in addition to the Ananda Publications business that published and distributed Kriyananda's works, as well as taped lectures and chants by Kriyananda and community members.

(5) Cultural transformation. As the revitalization movement becomes better adapted, "a noticeable social revitalization occurs, signalized by the reduction of the personal deterioration symptoms of individuals, by extensive cultural changes, and by an enthusiastic embarkation on some organized program of group action" (Wallace 1956, 275).

Through attempts to "live a simple life devoted to God," Ananda members vastly reduce the amount of stress in their lives and in their environments. When asked what changes in their own behavior they had noticed since joining the community, Ananda members responded with comments like "more empathy" as a result of "inner peace"; "I am more understanding and loving toward others"; "I rarely lose my temper, which was something that happened frequently; more open and able to show love to others"; "I used to be very introspective and non-conversational and though there's room for improvement, I'm much more open with others"; "less judgmental"; "becoming less judgmental, more loving"; "I am more dispassionate, less emotionally involved—kinder and more compassionate at the same time"; "more considerate, more sensitive to their feelings"; "I find it easier to be more understanding"; "more open, less selfish"; "I am less shy, more confident, mature."[8]

(6) Routinization. Through its political and social structures and its informal rules, Ananda can be said to have reached routinization. That is, its program has long been "established as normal in various economic, social, and political institutions and customs" (Wallace 1956, 275). Ananda's outreach programs and membership process bring new members into the fold and help them to make the transition necessary to live in the Ananda community.

Kriyananda did express concern when I asked him what chances Ananda might have of surviving his own death. He replied:

> The unfortunate fact is that organizations don't usually go, at least in the same way—they cease to be creative—after the founder dies. And they may endure, but they cease to be creative. I'm doing my best not to let that happen. But whether I

> will succeed or not, I don't know . . . The worry that I have is: will it be dynamic? As it stands now, most of the new influence comes from me, and I'm still very much the founder in the sense that it's an ongoing founding—ongoing creativity. And I hope that (because we do have creative people) that changes bit by bit. Because it's not as if they have to sit around waiting for me. But when I come on the scene, then suddenly I have ideas that make the new things happen. And the way out of that isn't to sit back and not have the ideas and force them to have them. It's to inspire them to the point where they don't need to come to me for the solutions. And I'm trying hard to make that happen. (Kriyananda 1986)

New Steady State

Finally, according to Wallace, a new steady state is achieved as a result of the cultural transformation brought about by the revitalization movement. The Ananda community itself has expanded, with successful colonies in Palo Alto, California, and Assisi, Italy. Ananda owns one of the largest New Age bookstores in the world, and its other businesses seem to be flourishing also. After thirty years of existence, Ananda can be said to have established itself within the larger society.

One measure of this is that Ananda has abandoned many of the markers that distinguished it from the society at large, because they are no longer necessary. Kriyananda no longer gives out spiritual names, and community members wear Indian clothing only on special occasions. Even Kriyananda himself has gone back to using his given name, James Donald Walters, on the books he writes.

But the point of the people who helped found and joined these communities was not only, as Tipton notes, to "get saved" from the sixties, but to reconstruct a society better than the one against which they had rebelled. Thus, the shortcomings of the larger society in the late sixties that led so many people to Ananda and other communities were rectified within these communities, often more quickly than in the larger society. And in the intervening thirty years since its inception, the larger society—in its awareness of the environment, in its recapturing of spirituality, in its emphasis on community, and in the ways its mainstream religions have changed—has actually moved closer to Ananda than the other way around.

Community building, revitalization, and cultural critique

The critique of American society that so many young people engaged in in the sixties made many valid points and led to many different kinds of revitalization movements. Ananda Village and some of the other communities founded during the latest communitarian phase in the United States have been relatively successful, because they fulfilled needs that the larger society could not fulfill, and they continue to do so. Their critiques of the larger society were significant.

Wallace notes, however, that not all revitalization movements are successful. Some are "abortive," with their progress "arrested at some intermediate point" (1956, 278). In fact, most intentional communities are short-lived and incompletely realize the visions of their founders. Even so, the study of these communities and the people who set about founding them can be instructive regarding the indigenous critique of the larger society.

Janzen notes the tendency for scholars, along with members of communities themselves, to give in to the "tendency to retain this concept of the commune as a closed unit" (1981, 38). Thus, Janzen explores "a model that focuses on the overlap between the communal society and the larger national society of which they are a part. This cultural intersection will be called the intentional community interface . . ." (1981, 39). This interface persists, according to Janzen, because the subsystems necessary for the operation of the intentional communities themselves "must not only be internally consistent but must also be compatible with the national system" (1981, 39). This insight leads to the recognition of a "duality" within the intentional community itself—it serves as a haven from certain aspects of social life of the larger society, but it must also exist within the broad outlines of that society.

The "intentional community interface" that Janzen mentions may, in fact, be the means of understanding why some communities succeed and others fail in their critiques. For example, I have already mentioned how economically successful Ananda has been. According to Janzen, "all intentional communities tied their economic subsystem to that of the national community. If this bond were sufficiently strengthened, a point could be reached where the economic interests of the communal society were the same as those of the national community" (1981, 40–41). Ananda members rejected the ethic of competition, which was characteristic of American society in the past, in favor of an ethic of cooperation. Both competition and cooperation allow for success in business enterprises; thus, Ananda's critique of competition does not prevent an "interface" along economic lines with the larger society but merely tempers the nature of that interface.

On the other hand, Josiah Warren's anarchist communities often failed precisely because they lacked a sufficient interface with the larger economy. Warren's innovative idea of using labor notes rather than currency in order to acknowledge the value of the labor put into a production worked only in a limited fashion, pointing out the shortcomings in some of his own critiques of the larger society (see Martin 1970). Warren had latched onto Adam Smith's labor theory of value (Smith 1981, 47)[9]—an erroneous concept later corrected by Carl Menger and the Austrian school of economics with their theory of subjective value (see Menger 1950).

A successful revitalization movement, specifically an intentional community, helps people to learn through experience—that is, through the juxtaposition of the new way of life with the old one that is the object of the critique. The intentional community interface provides a feedback mechanism between the community and the larger society, so that ultimately the critical juxtaposition disappears and the community becomes a bona fide aspect of the larger society that is integrated into the whole.

Conversely, an unsuccessful revitalization movement—one that fails in its critique with the larger society—might still juxtapose its way of life with that of the larger society, but the lack of a sufficient interface makes feedback impossible. Therefore, the community does not eventually become part of the larger society and is often threatened or destroyed by that society.

In much the same way, an epistemological critique can only be effective if there is a sufficient feedback mechanism that allows the lessons of the movement or community to be fed into the larger society, for the example of different ways of knowing is not enough. In the case of Ananda, its way of knowing through kriya yoga required a religious interface with the larger society. Because of the presence of similar strands of religious understanding, both in the history of the United States and in a large part of the population that did not belong to the community, Ananda's way of knowing acquired a certain validity that allowed it to become part of the religious mainstream, though it combined Eastern and Western thought in unusual ways.

Indigenous critique through revitalization—especially through the formation of intentional communities—is an especially significant factor in the study of complex societies that must maintain cohesiveness among millions of people. The study of these critiques allows us to understand the mechanisms through which large state societies change, maintaining coherence through the integration of the new that seems to work and is not completely out of alignment with what already exists. Thus, intentional communities constitute one more tool for the analysis of culture and society.

Notes

1. Wallace (1956, 264) actually mentions "utopian community" in the opening paragraph of his paper, along with other phenomena (for example, revolutions, social movements, and so on) that are usually not included in anthropology texts under the topic of revitalization, but which clearly share the traditional characteristics and processes that Wallace ascribes to revitalization movements.

2. For a history of the Frankfurt School, see Bottomore (1984).

3. Zablocki names the other periods the Shaker Influx (1790–1805), the Utopian Socialist Period (1824–48), the Turn of the Century (1890–1915), and the most recent period (1965-1976), which is the subject of his book (1980, 33–40).

4. Fieldwork at Ananda took place in the summer of 1986. Subsequent studies were carried out among Ananda associates in San Diego from 1986 to 1987 and 1987 to 1988. In addition to the help provided me by Swami Kriyananda and the entire Ananda community (including Stephanie, Evelyn,

Durga, Vidura, Terry, Devi, Jaya, Mark, Jay, Sudarshan, Savitri, Susan, Bob, Bent, Parvati, Shoshana, Karuna, Asha, and others who must remain anonymous), I wish to thank Vivian J. Rohrl, Edward O. Henry, Ann B. Cottrell, Wade C. Pendleton, Lawrence C. Watson, John R. Weeks, Stephanie Sandin, Dean M. Sandin, and Gertrude Sumner for their help with this project. A Claude R. Lambe Fellowship from the Institute for Humane Studies at George Mason University (Fairfax, Virginia) and a teaching assistantship in the Department of Anthropology at San Diego State University assisted me financially during the time when I was doing research and processing much of the data on which this paper is based.

5. By 1960 90 percent of all U.S. households had a television set (Strickland and Ambrose 1985). Television served as one of the great integrating factors for the baby-boom generation, exposing the 46 million members of its vanguard (those born between 1946 and 1951) to the same images, ideals, and experience of violence.

6. Kriyananda tells the story of his dismissal from SRF in his book *A Place Called Ananda, Part One* (1996).

7. All people were prohibited from using drugs or alcohol on Ananda property, whether or not they were members. However, Ananda members were prohibited from using drugs and alcohol whether or not they were on Ananda property. The rule against dogs arose to protect the many wild deer that roamed the Ananda property.

8. All of these quotations are excerpted from responses of Ananda members to a survey given by me in 1986. See Brown 1987 for details of this survey.

9. It is important to note, however, that Adam Smith did not employ the labor theory of value as naïvely as those who followed him. Although he did say, "The real price of every thing, what every thing really costs to the man who wants to acquire it, is the toil and trouble of acquiring it. . . . What is bought with money or with goods is purchased by labour as much as what we acquire by the toil of our own body" (Smith 1981, 47), he goes on to elaborate on the connection of this labor to the rest of the market system in a way others seem to forget. Thus, the attempt to translate labor into value via labor notes (the worth of which was usually calculated in terms of time) missed the point entirely.

Reference List

Alexander, Kay. 1992. Roots of the New Age. In *Perspectives on the New Age,* edited by James R. Lewis and J. Gordon Melton, 30–47. Albany: State University of New York Press.

Botscharow, Lucy Jayne. 1989. Disharmony in Utopia: Social Categories in Robert Owen's New Harmony. *Communal Societies* 9:76–90.

Bottomore, T. B. 1984. *The Frankfurt School.* New York: Tavistock.

Brown, Susan Love. 1987. Ananda Revisited: Values and Change in a Cooperative, Religious Community. M.A. thesis, San Diego State University.

———. 1992. Baby Boomers, American Character, and the New Age: A Synthesis. In *Perspectives on the New Age,* edited by James R. Lewis and J. Gordon Melton, 87–96. Albany: State University of New York Press.

———. 1999. Baby Boomers. In *The Sixties in America,* edited by Carl Singleton. Pasadena, Calif.: Salem Press.

———. 2001. God and Self: The Shaping and Sharing of Experience in a Cooperative, Religious Community. In *The Psychology of Cultural Experience,* edited by Carmella Moore and Holly Mathews. Cambridge: Cambridge University Press.

Cleçak, Peter. 1983. *America's Quest for the Ideal Self: Dissent and Fulfillment in the Sixties and Seventies.* New York: Oxford University Press.

Diem, Andrea Grace, and James R. Lewis. 1992 Imagining India: The Influence of Hinduism on the New Age Movement. In *Perspectives on the New Age,* edited by James R. Lewis and J. Gordon Melton, 48–58. Albany: State University of New York Press.

Durkheim, Emile. 1984. *The Division of Labor in Society.* Translated by W. D. Halls. New York: The Free Press.

Ellwood, Robert. 1992. How New Is the New Age? In *Perspectives on the New Age,* edited by James R. Lewis and J. Gordon Melton, 59–67. Albany: State University of New York Press.

Gitlin, Todd. 1987. *The Sixties: Years of Hope, Days of Rage.* New York: Bantam Books.

Haviland, William. 1997. *Anthropology.* 7th ed. San Diego: Harcourt Brace.

Jackson, Carl T. 1981. *The Oriental Religions in American Thought: Nineteenth-Century Explorations.* Westport, Conn.: Greenwood Press.

Janzen, Donald E. 1981. The Intentional Community-National Community Interface: An Approach to the Study of Communal Societies. *Communal Studies* 1:37–42.

Jones, Landon Y. 1980. *Great Expectations: America and the Baby Boom Generation.* New York: Ballantine Books.

K'Meyer, Tracy Elaine. 1997. *Interracialism and Christian Community in the Postwar South: The Story of Koinonia Farms.* Charlottesville: University Press of Virginia.

Kriyananda, Swami (James Donald Walters). 1977. *The Path: Autobiography of a Western Yogi.* Nevada City, Calif.: Ananda Publications.

———. 1986. Interview with Susan Love Brown.

———. 1996. *A Place Called Ananda, Part One*. Nevada City, Calif.: Crystal Clarity.

Lee, Dallas. 1971. *The Cotton Patch Evidence: The Story of Clarence Jordan and the Koinonia Farm Experience*. New York: Harper and Row.

Marcus, George E., and Michael M. J. Fischer. 1986. *Anthropology as Cultural Critique: An Experimental Moment in the Human Sciences*. Chicago: University of Chicago Press.

Martin, James J. 1970. *Men Against the State*. Colorado Springs, Colo.: Ralph Myles.

Menger, Carl. 1950. *Principles of Economics*. Glencoe, Ill.: The Free Press.

Nordquist, Ted A. 1978. *Ananda Cooperative Village: A Study in Beliefs, Values, and Attitudes of a New Age Religious Community*. Uppsala, Sweden: Religionshistoriska institutionen.

Oved, Yaacov. 1993. *Two Hundred Years of American Communes*. New Brunswick, N.J.: Transaction.

Riesman, David, Nathan Glazer, and Reuel Denney. 1950. *The Lonely Crowd: A Study of Changing American Character*. New Haven: Yale University Press.

Robbins, Thomas. 1969. Eastern Mysticism and the Resocialization of Drug Users: The Meher Baba Cult. *Journal for the Scientific Study of Religion* 8:308–17.

Smith, Adam. [1776] 1981. *An Inquiry Into the Nature and Causes of the Wealth of Nations*. Reprint, Indianapolis, Ind.: Liberty Classics.

Strickland, Charles E., and Andrew M. Ambrose. 1985. The Baby Boom, Prosperity, and the Changing Worlds of Children, 1945–1963. In *American Childhood, a Research Guide and Historical Handbook,* edited by Joseph M. Hawkes and N. Ray Hiner, 533–85. Westport, Conn.: Greenwood.

Thomas, Wendell. 1930. *Hinduism Invades America*. New York: Beacon Press.

Tipton, Steven M. 1982. *Getting Saved From the Sixties: Moral Meaning in Conversion and Cultural Change*. Berkeley: University of California Press.

Tönnies, Ferdinand. 1957. *Community and Society (Gemeinschaft und Gesellschaft)*. New Brunswick, N.J.: Transaction Books.

Wallace, Anthony. 1956. Revitalization Movements: Some Theoretical Considerations for Their Comparative Study. *American Anthropologist* 58, no. 2:264–81.

———. 1972. *Death and Rebirth of the Seneca*. New York: Vintage Books.

Warren, Josiah. 1852. *Equitable Commerce*. New York: Burt Franklin.

Whyte, William. 1956. *The Organization Man*. New York: Simon and Schuster.

Wunderlich, Roger. 1986. The Three Phases of Modern Times—Communitarian, Reform, and Long Island. *Communal Societies* 6:50–60.

———. 1992. *Low Living and High Thinking at Modern Times, New York*. Syracuse, N.Y.: Syracuse University Press.

Yogananda, Paramahansa. 1985. *Autobiography of a Yogi*. Los Angeles: Self-Realization Fellowship.

Zablocki, Benjamin. 1980. *Alienation and Charisma: A Study of Contemporary American Communes*. New York: The Free Press.

Contributors

JONATHAN G. ANDELSON, "Coming Together and Breaking Apart: Sociogenesis and Schismogenesis in Intentional Communities," is professor of anthropology at Grinnell College in Grinnell, Iowa, where he has taught since 1974. He earned his doctorate from the University of Michigan and has conducted ethnographic and historical research in the Amana colonies of Iowa and a Mormon community in Utah and has done archival research in Germany. His interest in intentional communities began in the early 1970s, and his studies of Iowa's Amana colonies have resulted in articles in *American Ethnologist*, *Human Organization*, *Communal Societies*, *The Palimpsest*, and *Communities* magazine. He has contributed chapters on Amana to Donald E. Pitzer's *America's Communal Utopias* (1997) and Timothy Miller's *When Prophets Die* (1991), and he wrote the entry on intentional communities for the *Encyclopedia of Cultural Anthropology* (1996). He is currently working on a book-length study of Amana history and culture. He is past president of the Communal Studies Association and currently serves as the book review editor of *Communal Societies*.

SUSAN LOVE BROWN, "Introduction" and "Community as Cultural Critique," is associate professor of anthropology at Florida Atlantic University in Boca Raton. She received her master's degree in anthropology from San Diego State University and her doctorate from the University of California, San Diego. She has conducted field research in Ananda Village, a cooperative, religious community in northern California, and in Cat Island, Bahamas. Her papers and book reviews have appeared in *Critical Review*, *PoLAR: Political and Legal Anthropology Review*, and *Communal Societies*. She has book chapters in Gordon Melton and James R. Lewis's *Perspectives on the New Age* (1992), James G. Carrier's *Meanings of the Market* (1997), Mimi R. Gladstein and Chris Sciabarra's *Feminist Interpretations of Ayn Rand* (1999), and Carmella Moore and Holly Mathews's *The Psychology of Cultural Experience*. She is co-author with Robert Bates Graber et al. of *Meeting Anthropology Phase to Phase* (Carolina Academic Press, 2000). She is currently a board member of the Communal Studies Association.

ELIZABETH A. DE WOLFE, "The Mob at Enfield: Community, Gender, and Violence against the Shakers," is assistant professor of American studies at the University of New England in Biddeford, Maine. She received her bachelor's degree in social science from Colgate University, her master's degree in anthropology from SUNY, Albany, and her doctorate in American and New England studies from Boston University. Her research on anti-Shaker writing was supported by a dissertation fellowship from the Pew Program in Religion and American History, research fellowships from the National Endowment for the Humanities, a research fellowship from the Winterthur Museum and Library, and the University of New England Faculty Research Fund. In 1995, she received the Starting Scholar Award from the Communal Studies Association, and she was recently invited to write an introductory essay to Absolem Blackburn's *A Brief Account of the . . . Shakers*, a previously unknown Shaker apostate account. Her papers and book reviews have appeared in *Religion and American Culture*, *Communal Societies*, *Teaching Anthropology, Maine History*, *Shakers World*, *The Shaker Messenger*, and *Winterthur Portfolio*. She has contributed a chapter to Nancy Schultz's *Fear Itself: Enemies Real and Imagined in American Culture* (1999), and is coeditor with Thomas S. Edwards, of *Such News of the Land* (2001).

LAWRENCE FOSTER, "Between Two Worlds: Community, Liminality, and the Development of Alternative Marriage Systems," is professor of history at Georgia Institute of Technology in Atlanta and a past president of the Communal Studies Association. He received his doctorate from the University of Chicago in 1976 under the direction of Martin E. Marty. A former Woodrow Wilson, Ford Foundation, National Endowment for the Humanities, and Fulbright fellow, he has written extensively on American social and religious history. His first book, *Religion and Sexuality* (1981, 1984), received the Best Book award from the Mormon History Association. It uses historical anthropological perspectives to analyze the introduction of new patterns of marriage, family life, and sex roles among the Shakers, the Mormons, and members of the Oneida Community. His second book, *Women, Family, and Utopia* (1991), further explores the impact of these three alternative communal systems on the lives of women and the implications that these experiments have for contemporary efforts to reorganize relations between the sexes. In his third book, *Free Love in Utopia* (2001), Foster edits previously inaccessible documentary material on the origin of the Oneida Community. Foster's strong cross-cultural interests derive in part from childhood experiences growing up in the Philippines in a missionary intellectual family, members of which cumulatively spent more than fifty years teaching in and exploring the twentieth-century cultures of China, Korea, Japan, and the Philippines.

LUCY JAYNE KAMAU, "Liminality, Communitas, Charisma, and Community," is professor of anthropology at Northeastern Illinois University in Chicago. She received her doctorate from the University of Chicago in 1971. She has been a member of the board of directors of the Communal Studies Association since 1992 and is its outgoing president. She has conducted research on the New Harmony community and related subjects since 1984. Her research has been funded by the Indiana Historical Society, the National Endowment for the Humanities, the Endowment for New Harmony Studies, and the Committee on Organized Research at Northeastern Illinois University. Her publications include *The Life of Symbols,* coauthored with Mary Lecron Foster (1990), and numerous journal papers and book chapters, including "Davy Crockett and Mike Fink: An Interpretation of Cultural Continuity," "Disharmony in Utopia: Social Categories in New Harmony, Indiana," "Neighbors: Conflict and Harmony on the Indiana Frontier," "Public Space in

Harmonist and Owenite Society," and "Nostalgia on the Wabash and Realism on the Ohio: Tourism, Official History, and Folk History." She is presently writing a monograph on the early history of the county in which New Harmony is located.

MATTHEW RENFRO-SARGENT, "The Borderlands of Communalism: Refugee Camps, Intentional Communities, and Liminality," received his bachelor's degree in anthropology at the University of Louisville, as well as his master's degree in sociology, concentrating on religious studies, social theory, and social movements as intersections into Hindu nationalism in the Republic of India. Currently, he is finishing his doctorate in sociology at the University of Kentucky, where he has published applied studies on the impact of welfare reform on Appalachian counties. Continuing his interests in social movements and nationalism, his current research involves education reform movements and the transformation of reform discourse from local interests to state manipulation as a form of nationalism. Ultimately, he wants to concentrate on nationalism and social movements as expressions in the struggle toward alternative forms of democracy.

GRETCHEN SIEGLER, "In Search of Truth: Maintaining Communitas in a Religious Community," is associate professor and chairperson of the social science program at Westminster College in Salt Lake City, Utah. She received her doctorate in anthropology from the University of Nevada, Reno, in 1992. Her areas of specialization include religious studies, utopian communities, social organization, and Caribbean studies. She is also the author of papers in Susan Palmer and Charlotte Hardman's *Children in New Religions* (1999), in Larry L. Naylor's *Cultural Diversity in the United States* (1997), and *The Anthropology of Consciousness, Special Edition #5* (American Anthropological Association, 1993).

Index